YOU GET WHAT YOU PITCH FOR

YOU GET WHAT YOU PITCH FOR

Control Any Situation, Create Fierce Agreement, and Get What You Want in Life

ANTHONY SULLIVAN

WITH TIM VANDEHEY

Library of Congress Cataloging-in-Publication Data is available for this book.

First Da Capo Press edition 2017
ISBN 978-0-7382-2006-2 (hardcover)
ISBN 978-0-7382-2007-9 (e-book)

Published by Da Capo Press, an imprint of Perseus Books, LLC,
a subsidiary of Hachette Book Group, Inc.
www.dacapopress.com

Editorial production by Christine Marra, *Marra*thon Production Services.
www.marrathoneditorial.org

Designed by Jane Raese
Set in 9.5-point Parable

LSC-C
10 9 8 7 6 5 4 3 2 1

FOR DEVON

CONTENTS

CAST OF CHARACTERS

When I came to America in the early 1990s I was, twenty-three, homeless, lived in the back of my van, and slept on top of boxes of mops. The only thing I had to keep me going was my pitch. Learning how to pitch has changed my life, and when I started working on this book, I looked for a way to talk about pitching that made it more than just selling or talking fast, which is how so many people think of it. It didn't take long to hit on what pitching really is.

Pitching is a superpower. Do it right and you'll change minds, open doors, get opportunities, turn adversaries into allies, make more money, and gain the kind of confidence that makes other people want to know you. Pitching is the power to persuade people, get them on your side, and get them to give you what you want, even when the odds are stacked against you. How could that be anything but super?

With that in mind, we've organized this book around the idea of superheroes and superpowers. As you learn the Pitch Powers, the superpowers that all great pitchmen (and pitchwomen) have, you'll run across all manner of fun, tongue-in-cheek superhero and comic book clichés, from origin stories to training montages to bumbling sidekicks. Just imagine the book as a colorful graphic novel—except that at the end, you'll be ready to get the job, the date, and the deal of a lifetime—and you'll be fine.

Before we get started, let's highlight a few of the characters you'll meet.

THE PERSUADER!

Pitching's greatest hero, the Persuader, shows up when things look hopeless (for example, when a job interview is about to go pear-shaped) to demonstrate how to use the Pitch Powers to save the day. He's square jawed, charismatic, and looks damned good in a tux . . . like someone I know.

INCOMPETENT SIDEKICK

Batman has Robin. Captain America has Bucky. Superman has . . . well, Superman doesn't have a sidekick, which makes him smart. Sidekicks exist mainly to get taken hostage and generally muck things up. They'll show up from time to time as reminders of traps you might find in a pitching situation, but that I'll tell you how to avoid.

WHAT WOULD BILLY DO?

Billy Mays (the original OxiClean pitchman) was my partner, my closest friend, and the most insanely great pitching superhero I ever saw. From time to time, Billy will pop up to share some pitching secrets that could help you turn a loss into a win.

INTRODUCTION

From Welsh Street Markets to Selling to Millions as the Face of OxiClean

As we begin, let me clear up a common misconception right off the bat.

Pitching is not about selling.

Pitching can be *used* to sell, but that's not the same thing. Pitching is more. Pitching is about *connecting* with another human being. It's about being authentic about your ability to meet somebody's need or solve his or her problem. It's about filling up the room with positive energy until the other person—a recruiter or judge or credit card service rep or whoever—is *delighted* to give you what you want. Become a master at pitching and you become a boss at three skills that can change your life:

1. Connecting with other people instantly.
2. Taking command of every environment.
3. Getting people to see you as the solution to their problems.

Pitching and the ability to persuade people to give you what you want—even if they started out regarding you with suspicion or even hostility—is *power*. It's figuring out what someone cares about and then caring about it yourself so you can give them what they need. It's engaging a person face to face and eye to eye so they feel like you're speaking directly to them, even if there are fifty other people in the room. It's turning a crowd of glowering strangers with their arms folded into a legion of fans ready to say yes enthusiastically to whatever you propose, what I call *fierce agreement*. It's the power to get the job, get the girl (or guy), get the part, make and save money, get better service, advance your career—do just about anything you want to do. Unless you live on an island or spend your days playing video games in your parents' basement, happiness and success in life depend on persuading someone else to give you something you want. You're constantly pitching, even if you don't realize it. If you walk into a Jeep dealership, you're pitching the salesman and sales manager, trying to persuade them to give you the best deal on a shiny new Grand Cherokee and the best price on your trade-in.

If you see someone interesting and attractive at a bar or nightclub and want to get their phone number, you're pitching them. You're trying to engage their sense of humor, get past their natural skepticism at being hit on, pique their interest, and build some trust so they'll take a chance on meeting you for coffee.

When you walk into your boss's office for your annual performance review, you're pitching her on how you gave the company amazing work during the past year and convincing her that you should receive a gold-plated review, a fat raise, and maybe that corner office that's been standing empty since last quarter.

If you're a server or bartender, you're pitching customers every time you clock in. You're talking with them, paying attention to small cues and body language, listening to their terrible jokes, finding ways to make them feel taken care of, and possibly acting as their therapist, confessor, partner in crime, or wingman for the evening. Why? So you can get a big tip, pay your bills, and afford a vacation to Mexico where somebody can wait on *you* for a change.

I'm pitching *you* in this introduction. It's true. I'm trying to connect and get you excited so you'll keep reading, and I'm using all my enthusiasm and boyish charm to do it. (It's a shame you can't hear my English accent, because it's dazzling.) If you've read this far without even realizing it, then it worked. That's the power of the pitch. The better your pitch, the better your outcome. But becoming a pitching superhero doesn't just happen.

OXICLEAN, BILLY MAYS, AND ME

Convincing people to give you what you want is an art form that takes charisma and confidence, but no great pitchman becomes great based just on those qualities. The good ones make themselves great with practice and discipline, mastering a series of skills that have proven themselves from the street markets of coastal England and the home shows of America all the way to the election stump. Those are what I call the Pitch Powers.

Think of the Pitch Powers as your version of Batman's utility belt: an arsenal of precision tools you can use to craft a winning pitch, rescue a situation that's going sideways, or get a conference room full of people cheering for you. They're the essential techniques I've learned in more than twenty-five years "on the joint" (pitchman-speak for the area where you're selling, where you try to attract customers), and they've taken me from selling £10 car washers in rainy Welsh street markets to selling to audiences of millions as the face of OxiClean.

If you know me at all, you probably know me because of OxiClean. After all, I've done countless commercials for the product and I wouldn't be here without OxiClean. That also means I wouldn't be here without Billy Mays, and while Billy is a book all by himself, a little backstory is in order.

The first time I saw OxiClean, it wasn't called OxiClean. I actually don't remember what it was called. It was 1993 and I was working a corner booth at the Miami home show, a twenty-four-year-old kid selling my Super Shammy Mop. Not far from me was this lady at her joint with this giant mound of white laundry powder that looked like a prop from the movie *Scarface*. While I was busy pitching mops, business was slow for her. Around the corner was an older pitchman named Max Appel, sitting with his wife, Elaine, selling rubber brooms. I liked Max. He was a genuine guy who always had interesting ideas and would always come over and say hi.

Max must have noticed this new oxygen-powered stain remover and seen something that I didn't, because before I knew it Max was sitting at the joint with the white powder, and now it was called OxiClean. It wasn't long before Billy Mays was on the Home Shopping Network (HSN) selling OxiClean, and then a few a months later Billy and Max had produced the first thirty-minute infomercial for OxiClean—with Billy as the pitchman! I vaguely knew Billy, but he was the right guy for OxiClean; he just nailed that pitch. It was trademark Billy: loud, positive, going a mile a minute with his classic catchphrases. If there was ever a match made in heaven, it was Billy Mays and OxiClean.

Part of being a pitchman is finding the hook, message, or "wow" factor that makes your pitch stick. Billy found out that OxiClean wouldn't just take stains out, but that certain things would turn white instantly the minute it touched them. At HSN, where he was already pitching Orange Glo furniture polish, Billy was able to hone his pitch for OxiClean. He would take a wedding dress, sneakers—anything that was normally white—make them pitch black, and then do these live demos and blow people away.

The lines he would come up with! "Powered by the air you breathe, activated by the water you and I drink!" "The power of bleach without the damaging effects of chlorine!" "It's like a white knight in shining armor!" "The Stain Specialist!" They were perfect, pitch perfect. In very few words he was able to clearly communicate what this amazing new stain remover was doing. "It's not clean unless it's OxiClean!" he would bellow.

Billy would go from a relaxed demeanor to soaring bird of prey in full flight, right there on live TV, firing off these great lines one after another. He'd put a scoop of OxiClean in a fish tank and the water would go from black to white. It was amazing. OxiClean sales at HSN went through the roof; it became their biggest cleaning product ever. The hosts would get excited and Billy would get louder and louder. But the magic was the method. Billy was a master at setting everything up so that OxiClean looked miraculous.

It wasn't long before HSN was ordering forty or fifty thousand units of OxiClean at a time. Max Appel and his family had found their man in Billy, and Max decided the next step for OxiClean was to get it on store shelves everywhere. For that, he needed a two-minute commercial as a promotional tool. That's when he called me. I had just started my production company, Sullivan Productions, and Max knew me for a very successful commercial I'd done for a product called the Tap Light. A meeting was arranged at the Venetian Resort Hotel in Las Vegas in

1998 and Max said, "I want you and Billy to work together and do a two-minute commercial." Billy and I looked at each other. At this point, we were not the best of buddies; we were rivals who didn't really have time for each other. I couldn't see Billy taking direction from me.

Finally, we agreed. One commercial. *One*.

Then, flying home from Vegas in first class, guess who was sitting next to me? I pulled out my laptop and asked Billy what part of his HSN pitches would fit into a 120-second commercial. We ordered a bottle of wine and he started pitching me, loudly, right there in first class, annoying the hell out of everyone. By the time we landed (after a second bottle of wine) we were half crocked, but I had this piece of paper with the best-of OxiClean lines written on it. I turned it into a shootable script, and a few days later Billy pulled up to my office in his Rolls-Royce. With a shoestring crew and budget, we set up a table and shot our first OxiClean commercial in three hours.

I was a rookie director and not sure how to direct Billy, who wasn't going to take any crap from me. He would glare at me as if to say, "Do *not* tell me what to do," but I knew what I was doing and he could tell I had our best interests at heart. To Billy's credit, he was a pro and he brought his "A" game; he was great at what he did. Me, I loved being behind the scenes, running the show, and giving him shit. He hated it, and he was constantly telling me to zip it and giving me the evil eye. That was the beginning of our back-and-forth relationship. The bottom line is that we both wanted it to work.

I edited the commercial in a day and sent it to Max for approval. He made one edit and it was done. We sent the commercial to the dub house for distribution to stations everywhere, and then it happened! You couldn't turn on the TV without seeing it. Suddenly, Billy and OxiClean were everywhere.

In a few weeks, we heard that the CEO of Wal-Mart, Lee Scott, was so excited about the spot that he made OxiClean a global VPI, a volume-producing item. Almost overnight, every Wal-Mart in the world had huge stacks of OxiClean by every cash register. In no time at all, OxiClean had gone from a small no-name brand to an HSN staple to the biggest thing to happen to laundry since bleach. I was walking down Madison Avenue in New York City a little while later, saw an issue of *Advertising Age,* and on the cover was our commercial! The best part, though, was that the guys from Procter & Gamble, who make Tide, had no comment.

After that, it was up and to the right. Billy and I shot more and more commercials—for Kaboom!, Orange Glo, you name it. We also became fierce friends. I loved it. I didn't have to be on camera. I could write and direct and Billy would go on camera and dominate. We shared in everything. He pitched, I produced, and it was perfect.

Of course, nothing that good could last. In 2005 I received a call from Joel Appel, Max's son: they had sold the company to Church & Dwight for $325 million. The next day I was in Denver and sitting down with the CMO, Bruce Fleming, who looked shocked when he said, "You're the marketing department for OxiClean?"

I told them that the marketing department was actually me and Billy. To their credit, they understood Billy's value immediately. They cut a deal with him, welcomed him warmly, stayed true to the pitch, and Billy and I were a team once more. For four years, we worked with the new OxiClean team and a super talented TV reporter and consumer advocate named Paul Moriarty to create many OxiClean and Kaboom! commercials. Then, out of nowhere, Billy died tragically in 2009, and after a very challenging few months, I ended up becoming the on-camera pitchman for OxiClean. I knew the pitch and knew the lines, and I've been privileged ever since to walk in Billy's very large footsteps. It's 2017, and my commitment to OxiClean and Church & Dwight is rock solid. So you'll be seeing my mug telling you how to get rid of stubborn stains for years to come.

I wasn't thinking in terms of Pitch Powers back in those days. We really didn't know what we were doing when we made that fateful commercial, but it's my favorite spot of those I've ever produced. The cadence, the offer, it's all perfect. In looking back, I realize that the key to pitching is to keep it simple. The Pitch Powers are really just good sense and knowing how to make people smile.

PITCH POWERS—ACTIVATE!

What are the Pitch Powers? I'm glad you asked.

1. **Know Your Acceptable Outcomes.** Before you set a toe in that office or walk on stage to give your speech, know your goals. What's the best outcome? What can you live with?
2. **Understand Their Pain (and Be the Cure).** Learn how your audience is hurting and why, and how you can help.
3. **Obsessive Preparation.** Know your pitch blindfolded. Practice until friends think you've lost your marbles. No stammering, no hesitation, just smooth, clean, and confident.
4. **Make an Entrance and Take Control.** Finally, you're ready to go into the room. When you do, make sure everyone notices. Use power words and gestures to

grab attention. Control the pace and rhythm. Stand out from everybody else.

5. **Breach the Force Field.** Most of us distance ourselves from other people for our protection. I call it the *force field.* If you can breach it with humor, compassion, or anything else, you can really connect.
6. **Facts Tell, Stories Sell.** Nobody wants to sit around a campfire listening to someone recite facts and figures about the stars and planets. But everybody loves a good story about the night sky. Tell a story and you'll have your audience in the palm of your hand.
7. **Love Your Mistakes.** You're going to forget details, get nervous, and otherwise step in it. You know it; so does your audience. Don't pretend. Use your flubs to get a laugh, break the ice, and make you more relatable.
8. **Push Back.** A pitch won't always go your way. The listener will dislike you, throw you a curve, or say no. Don't slink away; turn the twist to your advantage.
9. **Never Be Closing.** When you pitch, trying to make things happen can undo all the trust you've built and the spell you've cast. Don't force it. Don't close anybody. Trust the process, allow silence, listen, and let things happen.
10. **Finish with Confidence.** A great pitch ends with the listener wishing you weren't done. Accomplish that by making a confident exit or an impossible-to-refuse offer, until the listener can't wait to spend more time with you.

Since most encounters proceed according to a more or less predictable pattern, the Pitch Powers are meant to be used in a rough sequence: prepare, learn about your audience, make your commanding entrance, and so on. But as your skills improve, you'll find that you can improvise and mix them up to fit the situation.

Where to Use Pitch Powers

What situation? Any situation where you're across the table from another person or group of people trying to persuade them to do things your way, give you something you want, or agree with your idea—basically, almost every situation! People associate pitching with selling, and if you're in that line of work, you can absolutely use them to crush your sales goals, but the Pitch Powers are superpowers for a lot more.

Pitch Powers can become your secret weapon in areas of life where you wouldn't think knowing how to pitch would make a difference . . . but it does. What I'm going to teach you will help you:

- Land the dream job that seventy-five other people have interviewed for.
- Get the number of that attractive person who's shot down everyone else at the bar.
- Earn more tips than everyone else at your job put together.
- Destroy your sales benchmarks and earn bigger commissions than ever before while creating customers for life.
- Win a disagreement about anything, from where to eat to a child custody battle, without ill feelings on either side.
- Bring the house down with that big keynote speech or critical presentation.
- Get discounts and credit card rates that nobody else can seem to get.
- Talk your way out of a traffic ticket.

- Successfully make your case for that raise in pay or year-end bonus.
- Make an unbeatable case before a judge or mediator.
- Convince investors or crowdfunders to give their money to launch your start-up company or hot new idea.
- Convince your kids to do what you want without shouting.
- Become Teacher of the Year.
- Own the room at your next audition.
- Lead your team to the playoffs.
- Successfully run for office.

A few of the situations on that list probably apply to you. Maybe a lot of them. Either way, it's easy to see that being persuasive, charismatic, and confident can get you money and romance, open doors, get you out of trouble, and make life a lot easier. Pitching has brought me opportunities and gotten me out of a few scrapes, such as the time when, newly arrived in America and driving from California to the East Coast, I got pulled over and successfully pitched a highway patrolman a Smart Mop in lieu of a speeding citation that could have gotten me deported. Thank God that cop had dirty floors.

Pitching is powerful. But it's just as important to know what the pitch isn't:

- It's not a way to get people to buy things they don't want or need.
- It's not a con artist's trick. If you think that, you've probably been watching too much *Glengarry Glen Ross*.
- It's not a "say anything" weapon for getting someone into bed.
- It's not a secret tool for winning arguments with your significant other when you're the one at fault.

I'm going to teach you not to sell but to *share*. I'll show you why you can't persuade anyone until you love yourself. I'll impart trade secrets and explain the role that showmanship plays in a winning pitch. You'll learn to read your audience, control the tempo, win them over with total authenticity, and stop pitching at the perfect time to leave them craving more.

This takes resilience, repetition, and being best friends with risk. You'll get comfortable with rejection because no matter how skilled you are, no pitch works every time. But each time you go back to the drawing board and reassess what didn't work, you'll fine-tune it. Eventually, it will feel effortless. The perfect pitch is like beautiful music that you don't ever want to stop listening to.

I'm going to teach you how to be successful at whatever you want to do. You don't need a rich daddy. You don't need a degree. You don't need to rely on government handouts. You will need:

To work.
Take risks.
To smile more than you frown.
A strong heart.
Grit.
Determination.
Resilience.
To believe.
To get up early.
Chutzpah.
To be able to withstand extreme conditions.
To be able to laugh.
To be able to pick yourself up when you're down.

Can you do that? Then you can pitch. Forget about a magic word or getting bitten by a radioactive spider. Let's get you some Pitch Powers.

POWER NUMBER ONE

KNOW YOUR ACCEPTABLE OUTCOMES

Good for saving the day in every pitching situation.

ORIGIN STORY

It was Tuesday, June 22, 2009. I was sharing a limo ride to the NBC studios in Burbank, California, with Billy Mays and thinking, *Do not fuck this up* over and over again. I had been preparing myself for weeks for what was about to come, but I was nervous. After spending thousands of hours and most of my adult life pitching products on television, as well as making hundreds of guest appearances on every type of talk and news show you can imagine, I was going to make my first appearance on *The Tonight Show with Conan O'Brien*. I had been training, mentally and physically, as if I were getting ready for a big race. When the moment came for Billy and me to walk toward that famous curtain for our entrance onto the set, I wanted to feel ready. I had a few goals in my head:

1. Don't fuck it up.
2. Promote Billy's and my reality show, *Pitchmen*.
3. Increase my fame a little bit.

4. Look like I know what I'm doing.
5. Again, don't fuck it up.

One of my favorite lines from *Gladiator* reverberated in my head: *Win the crowd, win your freedom.* Right. It became a calming mantra.

You have to be a guest on *The Tonight Show* to fully understand what it feels like. You spend hours in the bowels of NBC, first in makeup chairs and then in the green room, before finally walking on stage in front of a live audience of millions. The show clock counts down to showtime: *tick-tock, tick-tock.* Can't back out now. Is this cold sweat normal?

Billy was already the most famous pitchman in the world, a booming-voiced icon in blue shirt and khakis, with jet-black hair and a jet-black beard, who had appeared on TV more often than Oprah herself. He had already been on with Leno twice, but this was my maiden voyage, and I went for a morning run in Runyon Canyon in the Hollywood Hills to unwind. Nearly twenty years earlier, I had come to America a nobody from England with less than $200 to my name. Yet somehow, I was a multimillionaire, about to appear on *The Tonight Show* with my friend and partner. I felt great and confident about our journey together.

We met back at the hotel. Billy had arrived late, but he was already in his blue-and-khakis uniform, and we ribbed each other as was customary.

"How many shows you gonna do today, Billy? Aren't we just doing the one?"

"I just want to give them options, Sul."

"What options? You always wear the same thing!"

"It's my suit of armor, Sul. How many times have I been on *The Tonight Show*?"

"Twice."

"How many times have *you* been on *The Tonight Show*? Oh, that's right, zero."

This was our normal routine, taking the piss out of each other. We'd had a lot of practice.

Ego Bomb

Soon after we arrived at NBC and were tucked into the green room, Conan's producer, Rachel, came into the room and greeted us. Then she said, "Okay, so here's the plan: Sully's sitting next to Conan."

If this had been a reality show, it would've been the moment when the camera zoomed in on Billy's face just as a thudding bass note played. It was like a bomb had gone off. Billy had a healthy ego and loved being a star, and he could go from teddy bear to super-pissed-off grizzly bear in the blink of an eye. Grizzly Billy was out. He glared at Rachel. Then at me. A grumbling "urgh-urgh-urgh" came from deep within the pipes of the loudest pitchman on earth, a baritone assertion that meant, *That ain't gonna happen.* You could've cut the tension with a knife.

Rachel began laying out the plan for our segment, but Billy interrupted her, pointing at his chest with his right thumb and saying, "I'm sitting next to Conan."

Without hesitation, Rachel fired back, "No, Sully's sitting next to Conan." So began the test of wills. I watched with amusement as the two of them battled like that, back and forth, for the next few minutes. Rachel wasn't giving any ground, so Billy finally played his trump card: he started putting his stuff back in his satchel like he was packing up, taking his ball, and going home. It was a bluff and I knew it. There was *no way* that Billy, who adored the limelight, was going to let me, his second banana, go on with Conan alone.

I understood why the producers chose to seat us this way, even if Billy didn't. They worried that with our healthy egos and Billy's louder-than-a-747 voice, we would shout over each other and turn the interview into chaos. If Billy sat next to Conan, they figured I would disappear entirely. They thought that if they put me between Billy and Conan, I'd have a fighting chance. What the producers didn't realize was that Billy and I were professionals. Over our two decades together we had become a well-oiled interview machine. We had our shtick down, and once cameras were rolling we knew how to handle each other.

When I realized that I was going to get the top seat, I turned my head to keep Billy from seeing my smile. Billy was pissed, and I wanted to stay out of the shit storm. But I was thinking, *I got him . . . for once!* My goals—my acceptable outcomes—for the evening, shifted instantly:

1. Don't fuck it up.
2. Get my brand and notoriety more on a par with Billy's.
3. Don't let Billy murder me.
4. Be charming and celebrity-like.

Then came the second blow to the man who built the house of OxiClean: Rachel told us that I would walk out first. Billy stared at her for several long beats and then just shook his head. After she left, I said, "Billy, you told me you wanted this for me. Well, here's my moment, and I'm taking it." That, I'm certain, is when Billy hatched his plan.

Billy did want me to have everything he had—money, fame, opportunity—with one exception: he absolutely did *not* want me or anyone else to overshadow him, ever. We settled into an awkward silence in the green room as he started doing his makeup. Billy did his own makeup, ironed his own clothes, did everything himself. It was part of his process. We watched Lisa Kudrow's interview and we knew Conan's team had us up next because, as the executive producer of *Pitchmen* told us, we had become a "world-class comedy team." We had the patter, the insults, and the laugh lines down to perfection. We would be doing a mock infomercial with a hundred products lined up on a table, and we didn't know ahead of time which ones Conan would ask us about. We had to be ready with our key lines and one-liners, and we were. We knew how to win over even the toughest audience and we weren't about to bomb on *The Tonight Show.*

Stealing the Seat?

Then Conan was done with Lisa and he threw to commercial. That's when the usher came to escort us to the curtained entrance that led to the stage. We got there and Billy gave me his big, warm Billy smile, a huge grin that seemed to stretch from one side of his big bearded face to the other. We fist-bumped. Then we were ready to go on and I could feel my heart beating out of my chest.

Once you're standing behind that curtain, you're in the belly of the beast. You're alone in the dark and can hear only the band. You see the images of bright lights through the curtain and feel the energy of the live audience. It's enough to take your breath away. Just the people who had appeared before us took my breath away. Barack Obama had appeared three nights after Billy's last appearance. We would share the stage with Elvis Costello, a rock legend in my house growing up. I couldn't help but think, *Holy shit, I've made it! I'm a lowly mop salesman from the boondocks of western England and I'm about to be on* The Tonight Show *with Elvis Costello.*

THE PERSUADER!

It's important to know your number-one goal before you go into any pitching situation so you can plan your initial strategy. That way, if you're met with obstacles, you can either adapt or go around them.

The Persuader says: "Let's say I'm taking my date to one of the most popular restaurants in the city. Even though I'm a famous superhero, I can't always get a table because I'm in my secret identity. So I go in with a plan: if the host tells me there's a two-hour wait, I'm going to inform him that a table near the kitchen will be fine. If he tells me that's not available, I'm going to tip him $20, which usually does the trick. In case even that doesn't work, I'm going to have a backup reservation and an Uber ride already lined up. Boo-yah."

The band wound down and we could hear Conan take over. Billy and I exchanged one more look. And that's when it happened. Just as I heard "Ladies and gentlemen, please welcome"—I felt a tremendous shove from behind and immediately thought, *You asshole!*—"Anthony Sullivan and Billy Mays!" All 250-pounds-plus of Pittsburgh brawler Billy had pushed me aside and stormed onto the stage in front of me. I couldn't believe I hadn't seen it coming, but it was no shock that Billy had done it. There was simply no way he was going to let me steal his thunder. I had to hand it to him. He knew exactly when to strike so that no one, including Conan, his staff, or me, could do anything about it. It was masterful timing.

The move actually put me in flight-or-fight mode. Being body-checked by a former football player just as you're about to go on national TV will do that. All my pre-show jitters evaporated. I smiled at Billy's back and thought, *Good one* as we made our way across the stage to meet Conan. Then I saw Billy eye the seat next to Conan: the hot seat!

Oh no, I thought, *he's going for it.* Billy *wanted* that seat. I saw him hesitate for half a beat, and I was sure he was going to keep up his silverback gorilla act. *He is going to hijack the seat next to Conan and there's nothing anyone can do to stop him!* My heart sank a bit but it also felt inevitable. But then at the last second, he veered left. Maybe he felt taking that seat would've been one bridge too far, or he was just messing with my head all along. I don't know.

All I do know is that Billy took his seat next to Lisa Kudrow, I sat down next to Conan, and we all settled in for the segment. Things went smoothly, we were our usual funny, horseplaying selves, and it was brilliant.

THE REVEAL

The thing is, even if Billy had taken the hot seat and I'd been stuck in the role of sidekick again, it would've been okay, because I had more than one outcome in mind for the day. The best outcome was what happened: I wound up in the star's chair next to Conan and got a boost for my brand and career. But if Billy had in fact pirated the right-hand seat and pushed me to the side man's spot, I still would've been on *The Tonight Show* and *Pitchmen* still would've received fantastic press. Even if the appearance hadn't gone well, I had a third outcome in mind: *don't fuck it up.* As long as I kept my cool and sense of humor, I would still have benefitted from the national exposure.

That kind of thinking is reflected in this Pitch Power.

KNOW YOUR ACCEPTABLE OUTCOMES

What are your goals for the situation where you're bringing your superpowers to bear? Do you know what you want to accomplish before you step into the office for the job interview? Before you sidle over to the bar to charm the attractive stranger? Before you walk to the podium to deliver a speech to your shareholders? And do you know how you'll react if one or more of those options is taken off the table?

Experience from English markets to US national TV has taught me that few things go according to plan. It's also taught me that the people who come out on top when things go sideways are the ones who don't have to get everything they want, just some of it. In other words, pitching stars don't let perfect get in the way of good.

Here's how.

Anatomy of a Superpower

I've started the book with this Pitch Power because it should be the first thing you look at when you're thinking about how to persuade someone to give you what you want. Before you research and prepare and learn about what the other guy wants, know what you want. Know everything that can come of the opportunity that you can consider a win. Each of those is an *acceptable outcome*.

True, some outcomes are more acceptable than others. You want to land the job, not get the cold comfort of being a finalist. But sometimes you won't get your first-tier outcome, and a lot of times it won't be because of anything you did or didn't do. If you're focused only on your first-choice goal, you could blow a solid secondary opportunity while you're busy being disappointed and pissed off. I've learned that there are few situations where you can't extract something of value—as long as you're prepared to do it ahead of time.

Using this Pitch Power involves a simple three-step process:

Step 1: Ask "What are my acceptable outcomes?" You saw that one coming, I know. But it's essential. What do you want to get from this encounter, date, speech, or sales meeting? What's the best outcome? Second best? Third best? Is there a second or third? Now and then, it's win or go home.

Let's take an easy example. Say you're knocking back a helping of Dutch courage before going over to speak to the lovely young woman seated alone at a corner table in a nightclub. She's already sent three stallions packing tonight, so you're nervous. But before you walk over, you sort through acceptable outcomes (or AOs):

a. Getting her number? Definitely. This is AO #1. We call this the *jackpot* outcome.
b. Getting your face slapped? No (unless you're into that sort of thing).
c. Having her agree to meet you here again later in the week? Sure. This is AO #2, the *runner-up* outcome.
d. Having a nice conversation and working on your game even though she's not interested? Yeah, that's not the worst thing that could happen. This is AO #3, the *honorable mention* outcome.
e. Getting your face punched by her boyfriend? That *is* the worst thing that could happen. Let's not go there.

So now you know what you're after, and having these outcomes in mind leads right to the next step:

Step 2: What do you need to do to reach each outcome? This is where locking in your AOs is such a smart move. If the object of your affection says, "I never give my number to guys in bars," most guys will wilt and slink away like kicked dogs. *Not you.* You have AO #2, and you say something like "That's all right, how about if we chat for a few minutes?" Odds are decent that you'll get a yes.

This step is about mapping out your responses should something come between you and each goal. It's a really simple formula:

a. Go for AO #1.
b. If blocked, ask, "Is AO #1 salvageable?"
c. If yes, switch tactics and keep trying.
d. If not, go to AO #2.
e. Et cetera.

If I take my date into a popular restaurant and they say they don't have a table, maybe I'll say that it's my girlfriend's birthday and I was planning on treating her to a $200 bottle of wine, or pull out an American Express Black Card. There's always a table somewhere, maybe reserved in case someone important shows up. Well, that's me. I just need to refuse to take no for an answer. If there really isn't a table to be had, what about a seat in the bar? Is that an acceptable outcome? Can I get a rain check and a voucher for a free bottle of wine when I come back? That's acceptable to me.

Step 3: How will I make the most of each outcome? Let's say my date and I end up in the bar, eating at a hightop table. Okay, I'm going to make that bar the spot to be in that restaurant, so that every guest hears how much fun we're having and wants to be where we are. I'll buy a round for the house, tip the bartender to let me go behind the bar and mix drinks, and maybe start doing a fake pitch of a Magic Martini Shaker or something. I have fun, make some friends, and let the restaurant manager know that next time, he needs to find me a table.

Every so often, there won't *be* a second acceptable outcome. Skydiving, for instance. *I'm kidding.* But seriously, when you're going after your dream job, not getting it but knowing that you made some great contacts is like being told "Great game" after you just struck out with the bases loaded in the last inning of the World Series. Sometimes the classic line is true: second place really means the first loser.

It's okay if you don't always have a backup outcome. Sometimes you're in a "go big or go home" situation, and that's cool. Give it everything you have and don't be ashamed of feeling

INCOMPETENT SIDEKICK: THE WHITE FLAG

You just went after your jackpot goal and hit a dead end. Shit. Okay, you regroup. But just as you're about to go back in after your runner-up, this asshole jumps in to surrender to the bad guys. That's what this loser does: tries to get you to turn tail and run as soon as you get some pushback. Don't pay him any attention, because you don't get anything you want if you give up. If you see something you want, go right at it. Plus, he's wearing a white flag as a loincloth . . . and nothing else. Yuck.

angry or hurt if things don't work out. That happens to everyone. Sometimes it's enough to know you bled for what you wanted and left everything on the field.

WITH GREAT POWER COMES GREAT RESPONSIBILITY

This Pitch Power helps you extract the most value from any situation where you're trying to persuade someone, but it has another benefit that might be even bigger. When you're not completely attached to your jackpot outcome, you're less worried about results, so you're more relaxed. Being relaxed makes everything, from sports to sex, easier. When it's not life or death that you get the client, you're free to focus on doing your best and just "grip it and rip it."

I can't think of a better example of this than Donald Trump. I can't read his mind and know what he was thinking when he decided to run for president, but I'd guess his thought process went something like this: *I probably won't win, but the worst thing that could happen is that I gain huge national publicity for my brand and my companies, so I make more money. If I win, even better!*

Of course, he did win, and I think he won in large part because of that "screw the outcome" attitude. In the beginning, he obviously didn't care. He was out to say what he wanted and have fun, outcome be damned, and that made his campaign fun to watch even when he was imploding. Trump was never boring, unlike every other Republican candidate. He called people out more than once and it was entertaining.

At the time, I thought, *There's no way the Donald is going to get away with this*. But he did, because he didn't care about what anybody thought and he didn't care about the outcome.

That freed him to be the opposite of politically correct at a time when conservative voters were furious about political correctness. You felt like at any time, Trump could've said, "You know, I've decided I don't want to continue my campaign. I'm going to focus on making America great again by building golf courses. Thank you." He would have stepped back after getting about a billion dollars in free publicity and gone back to his empire.

If you've spent your life white-knuckling outcomes in job interviews, sales meetings, or the dating scene, you've probably been limiting yourself and your results. It's human nature: when you obsess over an outcome, you act out of the fear that you won't get it. You don't act like a superhero. You're not aggressive or confident. You don't take smart risks. You play not to lose, and that's a great way to lose. Nobody punches above their weight in the dating scene, commission sales, or employment by going in afraid of failing.

Now, imagine if you had three or even four possible outcomes of a situation that were positive. Sure, you'd still love to hit the jackpot, but the world won't end if you don't. You can loosen up and play to win: gamble with bold statements or big promises, walk in super confident, tell jokes, or drop an f-bomb—whatever you need to do to own the room and control the tempo. Who knows? You might become president.

Not About Failure

When I talk about this Pitch Power, one of the objections I hear is that I'm teaching people to plan on failing when they pitch. Totally not true. Like I just said, knowing your acceptable outcomes is an *antidote* for failure because it expands your definition of success and takes away your fear. However, in some people's minds, the only legitimate version of success is one where you're crushing the world under the heel of your boot. They feel like admitting the possibility of failure is the same as failing.

It's not. That's self-help, motivational speaker propaganda. In the grown-up world, things don't always go your way. You don't always get the account. A wise pitching hero admits that sometimes, despite all your hard work, preparation, and ability, the decision does not come down in your favor. If you stick with an inflexible "win it all or take my ball and go home" approach, you're going to miss out on a lot of opportunities.

In a way, this is the old "expect the best but prepare for the worst" strategy:

- Do the work and bring your "A" game every time.
- Have additional AOs in mind in case you don't get what you want.
- Treat them as insurance. Even if things don't go perfectly, you have alternate means to extract value from the situation.
- You're protected, so go all out, be yourself, and don't worry about the result.

This is an odd example, but it works. Last year, I went to Burning Man for the first time. It was something I'd always wanted to do. But when I got dropped off at my camp in Black Rock in this sick, Mad Max–esque car called the Valyrian Steel (google it; it's insane), I was intimidated. Yeah, me. Mr. Pitchman, the Persuader. The camp had been going for three days and there were forty or fifty people there. I felt pretty out of place, but going in I had several acceptable outcomes:

1. Make lifelong friends and have an incredible time. This was my jackpot AO.
2. Meet some cool people and have an incredible time.
3. Not really meet anyone but have some awesome downtime from work.

None of those outcomes are bad, and the last was totally in my control. Even if I didn't hit it off with the people in camp and fellow Burners, I could still chill, relax, and have experiences. So I had nothing to lose. I walked into the camp and everyone was looking at me, so I went, "Hey everyone, I'm Sully!" and just stood there like an idiot. Everyone shouted, "Hi, Sully!" because that's the etiquette. Then someone came up and hugged me and said, "Welcome home," because everyone does that. Then (because I didn't already feel like a tool), I said, "Does anyone know where my RV is?"

Well, within five minutes I had two new friends, Niko and Ursula, and we were making drinks and meeting people and telling stories. I had an incredible time, in part because I went into the encounter with no fear about the outcome. No matter what happened, it would be good.

You don't need to go to Burning Man for this Pitch Power to save the day.

- **Negotiation.** This is the perfect match of Pitch Power and scenario. Whether you're negotiating for a car, a sales contract, or a book deal, having multiple AOs means you can be flexible, think on your feet, and outmaneuver the other party.
- **Any service situation.** Whether you're after a hotel room upgrade or a first-class airline seat, sometimes you won't

get your first choice. So have a backup. Can't get moved to a suite? Fine. What about a free breakfast or massage instead? No first-class seats available? All right. What about a bulkhead seat in economy so you have more legroom, or, if you have time, a first-class bump on a later flight? Don't walk away without getting *something*.

- **Selling.** The only thing people despise more than being sold to is a salesperson who won't take no for an answer. The solution is to play the long game. If you can't get the sale today, what can you get? If you're building a relationship (which, if you're a sales superhero, is what you should be doing), then maybe a second meeting would be an acceptable outcome. What about the prospect agreeing to let you send a written report on how you can solve his problems? What about a game of golf, no strings attached? You both know your long-term goal is to get the signature, so don't be clever. Go for the AO and build trust.

Story-Furthering Interlude

Scott Fairchild's living depends on having a lot of acceptable outcomes. He's a sports agent, representing world-class endurance athletes like triathlon legend and two-time Ironman world champion Chris "Macca" McCormack. And when he goes in to make a deal, he's been known to have as many as ten possible scenarios in his back pocket.

"My client might be the athlete, the event or the sponsor," he says. "I have to have multiple objectives in mind. First, you have to know what your goals are, what you'll accept. I'm the middleman, so I have to ask Macca or whoever, 'What will you take?' Then I have my scenarios. It can get complicated, because if I'm negotiating a sponsorship deal, there are a lot of ways my client can be compensated: salary, product, bonuses, years in the deal, exposure. I have to weigh all of that, plus the status of the athlete. Is he up and coming, in his prime, or heading for retirement?"

Scott cut his teeth working for Callaway golf, and he has a piece of advice that I really like. "Always say yes," he continues. "I might come in and say, 'We want four years for $1 million each,' and they might come back with, 'One year for $500,000,' but if I just say no and walk away, it's over. Always start with yes. I might say, 'Yes, we'll do that, but . . .' And then I'll propose that if my athlete wins X races, we get a $2 million bonus. I've got the if-then options memorized and we go back and forth until we get the deal done."

Scott has one more tip: aim high. "Always start higher in what you're asking for so you have room to come down," he says. "I always shoot high, and the people on the other side know my first number isn't what I expect to get. That's the game—and it *is* a game."

Plot Twist!

Naturally, no matter what you do, there will be times when every acceptable outcome falls off the table and you're left with nothing. Technically, these are called *shit storms*. In all seriousness, this kind of thing doesn't happen very often, but when it does, it's enough to shake the confidence of even a seasoned pitching champion. How do you handle it when you can't see a path to getting anything you want?

First, don't panic. Desperation never plays, and freaking out in an attempt to walk away with something—anything—will just lead you to make reckless offers and bad decisions. Look at the failure of all your AOs as a clear indicator that the opportunity, whatever it is, was a poor fit from the start.

Second, you can always salvage your dignity and professionalism no matter what happens. Even if the other party was uncooperative or hostile, you take the high road. Keep your cool, be gracious and polite, decline any offers that you find demeaning, and make your exit. Don't help the other party save face or avoid feeling guilty; that's not your problem.

Finally, if the situation is such a poor fit that you can't salvage anything, then maybe not hitting any of your goals is a blessing in disguise. If you really want a job, but at your interview you find out that your personality is a terrible fit for the company's culture, why would you want to work there? You'd be miserable.

It's rare to find a pitching scenario where you can't walk away with something worthwhile, like a key contact, a second appointment, or a referral. But it happens and it'll happen to you. When it does, don't be afraid to pull the ripcord. Remember, the opportunities that don't work out just clear space for the ones that will.

Training Montage

Learning to consider your AOs is relatively easy, because you just need to take some time before you enter the pitching arena and think about what you want. What's your ideal outcome? What would be okay if that didn't work out? If that runner-up fell through, is there a third option that could make the time pay off?

It's also smart to think about (a) possible obstacles and (b) your responses to those obstacles. For example, let's say you're shopping for a car and getting ready to pitch the salesman.

WHAT WOULD BILLY DO?

Billy Mays here! I was always a confident go-getter when I pitched; it was just part of my Type A, steel-town football player nature! I always assumed I would come out on top—but that's no excuse for not having backup plans, and that's what acceptable outcomes are. Back when Sully and I did *The Tonight Show,* I wanted the seat next to Conan, but if I'd had a "I've got to have his or the whole thing is ruined" mentality, I would've grabbed the seat, pissed off the producers so much they wouldn't ever have had us back, and maybe damaged my friendship with my best pal and partner. It's awesome to be confident, aggressive, and positive, but don't let those qualities keep you from being smart, too!

- **Possible obstacle:** the salesman trots out the old "What kind of payment are you looking for?" line.
- **Response:** "I'm not looking for a payment. I'm looking for a 3-Series at this price. Can we do that?"
- **Possible obstacle:** The salesman makes it clear the dealership *cannot* sell you the car according to the terms you want.
- **Response:** AO #3. You say thank you and go somewhere else. Don't waste any more time dickering.
- **Possible obstacle:** You agree to let the dealer's internal finance company compete for your loan but their terms stink.
- **Response:** You've already got approval from another lender and have the info on your phone. You say, "Give me the price I want and your finance company is not an issue."

Plan on what you will do under pressure. There's nothing more powerful than standing firm on your price or terms in any situation, whether it's a price on a car or a salary. What's your floor and are you ready to defend it? Have everything planned out, including the point at which you walk away. And forget memorization; put notes on your phone. Everybody looks at their phone constantly these days, so no one will think twice if you glance at your cheat sheet. That way, you'll be ready to pitch for the best possible outcome.

SCENARIOS FOR USING THE "KNOW YOUR ACCEPTABLE OUTCOMES" PITCH POWER

Q: *Your refusal to budge from a price or terms provokes the other party to become hostile. Do you react, sit silently, or leave?*

A: You wait, stay cool, and be the ball. That's a reaction to not being the one with the power, and if you wait, he or she will cool off and you can get back to business. Now you're in a position to say, "Okay, I really want to do this deal, so what if we did this . . . ?" And you turn to your next acceptable outcome.

Q: *You're negotiating in a field where you have little or no experience. Time to call on a good sidekick, like an attorney or agent?*

A: Definitely. Even if you can't have an expert with you in your meeting, you can get some information about the law, the politics, the money, or the players. And if you can invite your sidekick to the meeting, do it.

Q: *You've been thrown into a pitching opportunity with no time to plan or determine acceptable outcomes. Wing it and trust your X-ray vision to perceive the AOs, or just swing for the fences (and mix some metaphors)?*

A: This is a time to follow Scott Fairchild's advice about always saying, "Yes, but . . ." Be affirmative about wanting to do a deal, but aim high. Hesitation or appearing not to know your own value in situations like sales or salary negotiations will kill you. So do both: swing for the homer (aim high with your first request) but be ready to improvise a "yes, but" counteroffer when they push back, which they will.

POWER NUMBER TWO

UNDERSTAND THEIR PAIN (AND BE THE CURE)

Good for saving the day in job interviews, auditions, pitches to potential clients, sales meetings.

WHEN WE LAST LEFT OUR HERO . . .

You were sussing out your goals and acceptable outcomes, figuring out not only what would equal a home run from your particular pitching situation, but if you didn't hit it out of the park, what would let you walk out of the room with your head held high?

Here, we're still on pre-pitch prep. See, like I said, pitching is about way more than a great cadence and a few witty lines when you're on the joint. It's about preparation, preparation, and more preparation. Let's dig into your next pre-pitch Pitch Power.

Incidentally, there are a lot of stories about mops in this chapter, but don't worry. You don't have to sell mops to make this work for you. But if you have some sort of traumatic event in your past involving mops, consider this a trigger warning.

ORIGIN STORY

I'd had enough of the bone-chilling winter of 1993. I was headed south. Behind me was a grim, gray landscape and a season of the most epically shitty weather this English lad had ever seen—one nor'easter after another all the way from Detroit to Boston to Philadelphia. Ahead of me was Clearwater Beach, Florida. My partner, Swedish Mike, and I had spent months slogging through the sleet and slush, pitching products across the northern home-show circuit, when we got a call asking if we wanted to do a home show in Miami.

Let me think. I was twenty-four years old, had a van, money in my pocket, and was done with the cold. Hell yes, we'd work the Miami show! Florida had sun, girls, beaches, and no ice storms—I'd shine shoes with my tongue if I had to. We packed up our stuff, put Detroit in the rear view, and barreled down Interstate 75. We made Clearwater in twenty-four hours, and when we arrived, would you believe it was spring break? We were two European guys living in our van with a bunch of cash. Life was good.

One day, I drove by what was then called Home Shopping Club (now Home Shopping Network, or HSN) and thought, *That's where the real action happens*. It was pitching Nirvana, where pitchmen like Ron Popeil and Tony Little made more money in a day than I made in six months. *Someday*, I thought. *Someday*. Then I drove across the state to work the Miami home show. Miami was great, and we discovered that two weeks later there was another show in St. Petersburg. So we drove back across the state and camped out back in Clearwater waiting for the show.

I was on my joint working my "tip" (pitchman-speak for my crowd) and selling my signature product, the Smart Mop. While I was going through my pitch (spin the mop around like it's nothing, pile sand and ketchup all over the floor, pick it up, rinse it out, spin the head dry and drop it, toss it in a washing machine, slick as a magic show until the crowd's muttering, "Holy shit, if only mopping my floor was that much fun"), I noticed a woman who'd been standing in the back, watching me pitch three times. I'd "bally a tip" (get people to gather around me), make my pitch, sell some mops, leave everybody laughing, reset my stuff, and bally another tip, and she'd still be there.

This really annoys pitchmen. I might let you watch twice because you need a second dose of Sully to buy, but if you haven't bought by the third time, you're either a competitor, an IRS agent, or working with the INS. I didn't want anyone watching me, because people will record your pitch and "butcher" (steal) your intellectual property. I know because I used to do it.

I went right up to this lady and said, "I will not let you watch my pitch three times without buying."

She said, "I've been watching you."

"Who are you? A spyer or a buyer?"

"I'm a buyer for Home Shopping Club. You're good at this. You should be on TV."

I rolled my eyes. I'd heard this a thousand times. "If I had a dollar for everyone who told me I should be on TV, I wouldn't be working this show," I said. "I'm tired of hearing it. If I should be on TV, get me on television."

She didn't bat an eyelid, just handed me her business card: NANCY KUNI. "We've heard about this mop," she said. "I think it may be a good fit for us. We'll be in touch." Off she went, leaving me holding her card in my hand. I was stunned. I'd been waiting for the opportunity to connect with the Home Shopping Club and there I was, talking to a buyer, and I'd been a jerk. It was all I could do to keep it together and get back to selling.

"You Need Someone Like Me"

Fortunately, Nancy saw beyond my rude-boy obnoxiousness, and two months later I was sitting in the office of Home Shopping Club's VP of Programming, Jeff Shimer, wearing maybe $30 worth of clothes and trying not to wet my pants.

When I drove my van onto the HSC parking lot that day, my mind was racing. *I'm not going to get a second chance at this. This is the one job interview that I cannot fail. I have no television experience. I have no idea of what's going to happen. But I really, really want to be on television.* I knew that Nancy had said enough good things to get me a sit-down with a guy who probably didn't want to hire me. I also knew that if I was going to make this happen, I had to make him want to hire me. I had to deliver the pitch of my life.

Jeff was filling out a bit of paper when I sat down. He kept me waiting for a minute, then lowered his glasses, looked me over through narrowed eyes, and said, "So you're the mop kid, huh?"

You're on, Sully. "Yeah." A wit like a steel trap, ladies and gents!

"I've got thirty-two professionally trained show hosts downstairs. I've been told that I need you to sell this mop. I don't understand why I need you. Why do I need you?"

A beautiful question. A layup. I could see that Jeff saw me as nothing more than an interruption, but I was about to turn that around. I said, "How many mops have you bought?"

"Five thousand."

"Five thousand? That's $100,000 worth. That's a lot of mops." This was my moment, and I leaned forward in my chair.

"Jeff, you don't need me, but you need somebody like me. As far as I know, there's about five of us in the country right now who know how to sell this mop, and the other four live in LA. I'm the one sitting in front of you. If you don't use me, I will recommend someone else. I'll even give you one of their numbers, and you'll need to call them, because you will not sell five thousand mops without one of us."

Jeff blinked. I could tell I had him "under the ether" (pitchman-speak for having your audience under your spell), so I pressed on.

"All I do is sell mops," I said. "I live in my van down at the beach in Clearwater, and I sleep on top of these mops. For the last three years, all I've done is sell mops. I make my living selling mops. I live, breathe, eat, sleep these mops. Your show hosts, I'm sure they're highly trained, but I GUARANTEE you that they will choke on the air today if they try to sell this mop. There's a pitch, and I know it. I've got the secret sauce!"

You're familiar with the term *pregnant silence*? I knocked up that silence and left it there, filling that office. After a beat, I went for the close. "I think I'm your best option. It's your call." God, the nerve of me, a snot-nosed little shit, telling this industry giant what was his call! But Jeff picked up the phone, called down to someone in the on-air department, asked if there was any airtime for the next day, hung up, and said, "Be here tomorrow at twelve o'clock. You're on the air at twelve-thirty."

I said, "All right," and left.

To this day, it's the best pitch I've ever delivered. I did what Jeff couldn't have anticipated: I didn't sell him. *You don't need me. You need somebody like me.* There was no way I was leaving that network without getting a yes, and I got it. It changed everything.

THE PERSUADER!

You have a prospective client coming to town for a presentation and you really want their business. But things are really busy, so you decide to wing it and rely on your native charm to win them over.

The Persuader says: "Wrong! A great pitch begins long before they sit down with you. It's your job to blow them away. Make sure the airport welcome signs say WELCOME! with the company name. Learn if they, their spouses, or kids have birthdays around your meeting dates and get great gifts. If they're from LA, have copies of the *Los Angeles Times* in your office. If they're from Boston, have the *Boston Globe*. If they're from Atlanta, have the *Journal-Constitution*. This isn't butt-kissing. It's showing them that you care enough to invest the time learning what they care about. Trust me. This works."

I drove away, my mind going a billion miles an hour. *What the hell? I'm going to be on television tomorrow! I've been pissing and moaning about this my whole life, and now I'm about to play in the Super Bowl!*

THE REVEAL

I was confident, even arrogant, when I pitched Jeff, but that wasn't what got me my shot on HSC. It was my Pitch Power.

UNDERSTAND THEIR PAIN (AND BE THE CURE)

I knew something about Jeff's business and the problem he had on his hands with all those mops in inventory. In fact, I knew his problem better than *he* did, because he didn't understand that his usual hosts didn't have a snowball's chance in Miami of selling five thousand mops. The Smart Mop was a classic street market pitch—an old-fashioned "take it apart, whirl it around, show it off while wowing the ladies with a twinkle in your eye" busker's pitch. A smiling TV host who spent most of her time selling jewelry to old ladies would blow it. HSC would be stuck with unsold inventory, and direct-response merchants *despise* unsold inventory. They want to turn and burn.

I knew that, I told him, and he knew I was right. In the very next sentence, I told him that I was the solution to his problem. Then I told him that if he didn't want me, I knew a few other pitchmen who could sell the mops, too. This told Jeff that I wasn't just out for myself; I really wanted to cure his pain. I said it all with a lot more confidence than I felt, and Jeff respected my chutzpah enough to say yes. A few million products later, I'm still with HSN.

An old marketing adage goes "We do business with people we like." That's true, but who do we like? Among other things, we like people who "get" us, who understand the challenges we face, appreciate what we go through, and empathize with our troubles. That's what this Pitch Power does, but that's not all it does. I might like you and think you're a swell person, but that still won't make me want to hire you or give you money. There's more to it than just knowing about somebody's company.

Anatomy of a Superpower

There are actually three parts to this Pitch Power:

1. Know what the other guy cares about and let him know you know.

2. Really understand what troubles, frustrates, or burdens him.
3. Offer a solution.

1. Know what the other guy cares about and let him know you know. This one is simple. I've done it for years. Back when I traveled around to home shows, when I was in Philadelphia, I talked about the Eagles or the Flyers. When I went to Boston, I talked about the Red Sox or the Bruins. In Detroit, I talked about the Lions and Red Wings.

When I sold in Greenville, South Carolina, I didn't talk about Ford Motor Company, because five minutes of research told me there was a BMW factory there and many people in town worked in it. So I worked the factory into my pitch. I'd say, "I hear there's a BMW factory close by, so I know you all get big discounts on BMWs. I'm very happy that everyone in Greenville drives around in a BMW. That means you're wealthy, so having a $20 mop isn't a big deal, because you're all willing to pay for quality. You drive the ultimate driving machine, and now you can own the ultimate mopping machine."

This always got a laugh. We all knew it wasn't true, but that didn't matter. I connected with them over something they all shared. I wasn't giving them the identical pitch I'd just delivered in Raleigh.

Know who you're talking to. Before you go to a job interview, to speak to a professional group, or make a sales call, do your research. A great example of the power of this is my story of the Cuban mop. (*More mops, Sully? Yes. I told you I had a lot of mop stories, but they're relevant, so bear with me.*) I would go to home shows in Miami, but the Cuban ladies would never buy from me. I couldn't figure it out. Then one day I got smart: I asked a customer if Cubans used a different kind of mop. The lady smiled and showed me a Cuban mop—and it was a towel on a stick!

That's it. It's a T-shaped stick. You just wrap a towel around it, or if you really want to make it authentic you put a little hole in the middle of the towel and swirl it around the end of the stick. When you're done mopping, you just put the towel in the washing machine. You don't even have to touch it, and it cleans a giant floor area.

That's what was killing my sales. A damned towel on a stick. I would bring out a sponge mop and show why the Smart Mop was better. I would bring out a string mop and do the same thing. But the ladies loved their towel on a stick, so I had no credibility. But instead of giving up, I saw this as my chance to make that crucial connection.

The next day, I went back to my joint and was doing my pitch with the usual gaggle of Cuban ladies standing there, unimpressed. Finally, I looked at them and said, "What's the problem with you ladies?" Then I went into my demonstration. I demoed the sponge mop. *Nothing*. I demoed the string mop. *Nada*. Then I pulled out a big towel on a stick. Every Cuban roared. Instantly, they were with me. They loved that I had figured out how they lived and what they used. I also learned how to pitch in Spanish a little bit—"smart mop" is *trapiador intelligente*—made fun of my own ignorance and worked it into my pitch, and sales went crazy. Those ladies still thought the Cuban mop was better, but they were walking away with my Smart Mop in their hands and I had their $20.

Why? I took the time to get to know them, and they loved it.

2. Really understand what troubles, frustrates, or burdens him. This second part takes more work and deeper thinking. It's not enough to memorize facts about your audience; you need to feel what keeps them up at night. Even if it's something that seems trivial to you, it's not trivial to them. It's not enough to know that a tech company is losing business because its products are outdated. You need to empathize with the owners—to know they're worried, because if things don't get better they're going to have to lay a lot of people off. When they sense that you understand why they're scared, angry, or exhausted, people will really tune in and pay attention to what you have to say. That's what worked for Trump.

No more mops—for now. Instead, think about radio host and financial guru Dave Ramsey. He's built a national brand, speaks all across the country, and has a devoted audience of millions. Is that because he's a financial genius? No. You can hear the same advice from half a dozen other people and read it in *Kiplinger's*. People love Dave because years ago, he got himself buried in debt and went bankrupt. He's talked about it openly. His listeners know he's not some Wall Street stock trader. He's made mistakes. He's faced a mountain of debt and had to dig his way out. He's one of them.

Dave Ramsey could've kept his past quiet. He could've packaged himself as a financial genius with no flaws. But he's smart. He knows nobody relates to that guy. So he turned his past into an asset: a way to let his audiences know that he gets them and feels their pain.

3. Offer a solution. Knowing your audience and understanding why they hurt are both crucial. But this Pitch Power is "understand their pain (and be the cure)." I'm not talking about the band The Cure, either. What puts you over the top is holding up your hand and saying, calm as God, "I think I have your answer."

Two years ago, I got a phone call from a former HSN buyer who had gone on to work with Nutrisystem. She had watched my production company go from zero to sixty in no time, and now Nutrisystem was searching for a new company to produce its television advertising. She thought I should throw my hat into the ring. This was exciting but intimidating.

Nutrisystem, as you probably know, is one of the biggest players in the food delivery–weight loss space. Their executives would be seeing presentations from the cream of the New York advertising world, agencies with Madison Avenue addresses that would land armies of people on the beaches of Fort Washington, Pennsylvania, bearing Euro-names and wearing black turtlenecks. Then there would be me, Sully, the OxiClean guy.

I knew that Nutrisystem had a healthy respect for direct response, but I also I figured they would have a healthy dose of skepticism about what I do, because some of my work falls into the "cheesy" infomercial category. But I also knew that *they* knew I could move the needle—that I knew how to sell—and that they were smart enough to care more about results than anything else.

You've heard of a "puncher's chance" in boxing? Well, as far as I was concerned I had a pitchman's chance, and that's pretty good. Plus, if I got the account it would be great for business.

I agreed to give it a try and went to work.

I had watched Nutrisystem's advertising and I knew what I was up against: big ad agencies with big budgets. But the problem with big agencies is that they approach every client the same way, like a guy trying to get a beautiful woman into bed by showing off his Ferrari. They make it about style, not substance. Agencies talk about how they need to "elevate the brand." I wasn't going to elevate the bloody brand. I would keep it simple. I would talk about *selling*.

My plan was to walk in with hard numbers and specific strategies and pitch Nutrisystem's pants off. I had little to no experience with weight loss, but I know what it's about: *looking good naked*. That's pretty much the bottom line, isn't it? For the average person, after you hit about twenty-two, looking good naked is a battle. I would pitch what I was good at: back to basics. I would break the ice. Have a conversation. Build a relationship. Leave without the order but play the long game.

My good friend Paul Moriarty came along with me and we set up in a meeting room. Then I couldn't get my PowerPoint presentation to work, and there was no place to plug in my MacBook. *To hell with it.* I pulled out a few sheets of paper and pitched the ABCs of what makes a great direct-response commercial. In my experience, a lot of companies get lost when they complicate what is a simple process. Their agency will tell them, "You need to get away from pitching. You're beyond that. You've grown." Wrong. The object isn't to win creative awards for your agency; the object is to sell. I told Nutrisystem, "You don't need to get away from pitching. You need to go back to pitching. You need to get back to basics. Get people to get off the couch and pick up the phone. What made Nutrisystem great in the beginning? Go back to that." I gave them a solution.

The Nutrisystem team got what I was saying right away. "Yes!" they said. "That's what we need, back to basics." They came to Tampa and we shot a commercial for them, but the magic happened when we worked on Nutrisystem for Men. I wrote the script and I definitely got back to basics: "Hey, guys,

INCOMPETENT SIDEKICK: YES-MAN

Yes-Man will get you into trouble by agreeing with everything the other person says, even if it's a terrible idea. Whether you're interviewing for a job or pitching a script, your audience doesn't want their own ideas regurgitated back to them, and they don't want you to be just like everyone else. They want guts and original thinking. They want to be challenged. Throw Yes-Man into the pit of burning acid, then tell them that you don't think their ideas will work—but you know something that will.

can't get into your pants? Got a beer belly going on? I've got one word for you, Nutrisystem. Put down the pie, get off the couch, pick up the phone and call Nutrisystem today."

It was straight talk, pitch talk. It's a very simple commercial, probably the simplest commercial I've ever written. If you watch cable news, you've seen it. I don't know why it's so good. I wish I did, because I'd do the same thing every time. But it's a knockout hit, and our relationship with Nutrisystem has been a win for them, for us, and for their customers. I even got to direct the great Dan Marino!

Understanding the other person's pain and dreaming up a way to fix it tells them that you care enough to put in the time. That you're mature and perceptive enough to stand in their shoes. That you're not just delivering a canned pitch that was the same yesterday and will be the same tomorrow. We live in a world where nobody listens; we're all too busy staring at our phones. This Pitch Power lets the guy on the other side of the table know you're paying attention.

WITH GREAT POWER COMES GREAT RESPONSIBILITY

There's no situation in life where that kind of meaningful connection won't help you get the kind of outcome you're after. But it's extra handy in circumstances where the audience might see one person after another after another for hours (or even days), until the candidates become a blur. You'll find that frequently in interviews for sought-after jobs and open auditions for paying acting gigs.

What people usually forget is that after enough time, the people asking the questions in those situations are begging someone to stand out and solve their problem. They're tired, bored, and hungry and they're dying to tell someone "You're hired!" so they can high-five each other and go home. Remember, the guy across the table isn't jerking you around or making you answer awkward interview questions because he's a sadist who likes torturing people; he *wants* to find someone who can meet his needs. Why walk into the conference room or walk onstage as one more anonymous face, praying they'll choose you, when you can make it impossible for them not to choose you? One way you do that is by coming to the table with ideas and answers that nobody else has and that you tailor to your audience.

Forget interviews and auditions—let's talk about selling. If you've ever sold anything, you've encountered sales resistance, that suspicious narrowing of the eyes and tightening of the voice that come when someone knows you're going to try to convince them to part with their money and buy something they probably don't want. Overcoming sales resistance with brute force is brutally hard, but there's a way to make it easier: make yourself a solution, not a salesperson.

I can't tell you how many times I've pitched someone that my entire goal for the meeting was to share information I knew they would value. That was it. I didn't care if I walked out with a signed contract, and I usually didn't. But I made myself a little bit indispensable. I offered ideas and expertise and didn't ask anything in return. People love that. I built trust and polished my reputation as an expert. More often than not I would get a return invitation, and at that meeting there was a better than fair chance that I would get the sale.

Selling this way is playing the long game. It's not going to give you the quick buzz of a fast commission. It's growing relationships, not writing orders. But that's why it works. If everybody else is coming in with the same canned pitch and call to action, be the one who offers great, workable ideas, no strings attached. They'll remember you, appreciate you, respect you, and in the end, buy from you.

Other scenarios where this Pitch Power helps good triumph over evil:

- **Vying for a raise or promotion.** What better way to prove your value than to dig deep into your employer's operations and come up with an innovative way to save or make money?
- **Trying to get the seller of a home to accept your offer.** It's not uncommon for prospective buyers to write letters to sellers to sway them in their favor. Try it, but don't be generic. Learn about the history of the house and the neighborhood and refer to it specifically. If your realtor has shared a challenge that the seller is facing, try to offer a mutually satisfying solution.
- **Pitching a literary agent.** Writers' conferences frequently have "speed pitch" events: you get five minutes with a New York literary agent to convince them to represent you and your book. Know the publishing world, know

the agent, and make your pitch about them—how you can make them money, make their job easier, that sort of thing.

Plot Twist!

However, if there is one thing I've learned on my journey from street markets and county fairs to corporate boardrooms and VIP suites, it's that nothing goes as planned all the time. The risky part about strutting into a meeting, sure that you bring with you the answer to all your audience's problems, is that sometimes, despite all your work and research, your answer is *dead wrong*. Embarrassingly wrong. Two seconds from being escorted out by security wrong.

How do you keep a miscalculation from becoming a catastrophe?

- **Be extra conservative.** Do extra research. Spend more time if you can get it. If you're not 100 percent sure that your ideas will be well received, don't share them. You might still get what you want anyway based on your presence and personality. Read the room (it's hard to do when you're nervous, so give it time): based on what you know, are the people you're pitching likely to respect your effort even if your ideas are off base, or will they be offended? Trust your gut and act accordingly. (By the way, that's just one of a hundred snap judgments that you'll become better at the more you pitch. Like most things, they take time, but eventually they become a reflex.)
- **Have a Plan B.** Come to the table with more than one idea that addresses the pain of the company or individual you're pitching. That way if one gets you the stink-eye,

WHAT WOULD BILLY DO?

Billy Mays here! What would I do if I found out in the middle of a pitch that the ideas I worked so hard on were circular file lining? One thing I wouldn't do is fake my way through it. The person sitting across from you might have been born during the day, but it wasn't yesterday. First, I'd own up: "Bill, you know what? You're right. That wasn't the right idea for you. My bad!" Then I'd pivot. I'd think fast and use what I'd learned during the meeting to come up with a new idea on the fly. People love people who can admit mistake, shake it off, and rebound with something creative. When I'm up against a wall, that's when Billy Mays performs best, and so will you.

you can pivot to something different. This is common in situations where a contractor is presenting a creative idea: a logo, an ad campaign, or a landscape design, for instance. If you're a smart professional, you will have Plan A, but if the client looks like she's about to come unglued at your first idea—voila! You whip out Plan B and with a little luck, the day is saved.

- **Push back.** I'll address this in greater depth when we talk about the Pitch Power, but for now it's enough to know that sometimes, the person on the other end of the exchange will either be wrong or testing you. In either case, the question usually isn't whether or not your idea is a good one but how firmly you believe in it. Take a page out of the traditional sales handbook and anticipate objections. Why doesn't your approach work? How could you improve it? Could you work on developing your ideas further and schedule a second appointment? In my experience, almost any situation can be spun into an opportunity provided you have the confidence to do so.

Training Montage

When I was working the gray, sodden weekend markets of England and Wales, all I had was my general knowledge of the "punters" (English pitchman-speak for customers) who came to shop for tea towels and buy socks from the usual group of traders. They were typically working class and tight with a quid, but receptive to a clever line and a bit of patter. That was all the research I could do.

You can do a lot more. As you're working to develop this superpower, research is your secret weapon.

- **Begin with Google.** Whatever the pitching situation, find and read everything you can about it and the people involved. Read company websites, newspaper articles, shareholder reports, and Yelp reviews.
- **Talk to live people.** This is where we separate the men from the boys. Too many people stop at online searches and chicken out at calling casting directors, ex-employees, journalists, or customers. But your mission is not only to learn facts but to get inside the other guy's problems, and the best way to do that is to talk with people who know what they are. Do *not* skip this step. A few calls and a few beers could yield information that will change your life. Pitchman tip: spend extra effort to get face time with people who are true insiders. Not everybody's information is of value.
- **Learn the business.** You might have written a terrific screenplay, but if you pitch it to a producer without

knowing that the last four films in the same genre were box office flops, you're going to look like an ass. Whether you're buying a car, making a speech, or asking out an attractive co-worker, know the backstory and the lay of the land.

- **Uncover the feelings.** We think we're all rational, but emotions are what really motivate our actions. The pain or frustration that your audience is feeling? That's what they want you to fix, even if they don't know it. Is your audience desperate for an innovative idea for a tech product? Bored with every guy who's fed her a line at a club? Angry at sales reps who've tried to manipulate them? *Situation + emotion = problem.* Fix the situation and change the emotion and you're a hero.
- **Have a plan.** You could sit down across from the CEO of a big company and say, "I know how to fix your business." But then there's the whole "escorted out by security" thing. Once you have facts, empathy, and an idea, a solution means having a detailed plan of limited scope. Don't try to fix the whole world; fix one commercial, product, or deal at a time. Be specific about how you'd do it. Explain why you *can* do it—and why you're the only one who can. If the other person asks for more details, that's a good sign. Get more time and get back to them.

But maybe more important than all of these is this: keep your eyes, ears, and mind open, always. You have no idea when pitch-perfect facts will appear; I've picked up intelligence that gave me an edge on the competition in everything from reading random newspaper articles to accidentally eavesdropping on conversations at restaurants. Useful information is everywhere, and it's all fuel for your Pitch Power. Use it.

SCENARIOS FOR USING THE "UNDERSTAND THEIR PAIN (AND BE THE CURE)" PITCH POWER

Q: *A new information source about someone you're about to pitch pops up out of nowhere and you're not sure it's reliable. What do you do?*

A: In my experience, having bad information about a prospect is worse than having none. So don't believe everything you hear, especially in this era of "fake news" on social media. Unless the source is someone you know, disregard it.

Q: *Your bold, risky solution to a company's or customer's problem falls flat midpitch. The person says, "That's really not an issue for us." Oops. How do you recover?*

A: Highlight the effort, not the outcome. "Well, even if I got the details wrong, you can see that my intention there was to be a problem solver. Everything I do is about making things better for you. That's how I do things—service, service, service." Who can dislike that?

Q: *The person you're pitching is a cipher. Despite your best efforts, you haven't been able to find out a thing about him or her. Does this Pitch Power still work?*

A: Sure! You just have to do your research on the sly. "Paul, I like helping other people solve their problems. Tell me, what here at Company X keeps you up at night? What are you guys most worried about? Because I think if I knew, I could really help."

POWER NUMBER THREE

OBSESSIVE PREPARATION

Good for saving the day in annual reviews, sales meetings, waiting tables—pretty much any pitching situation.

WHEN WE LAST LEFT OUR HERO . . .

You were working on ways to be the answer to your audience's pain. Well, as we discussed, a big part of doing that involves preparation. But in this chapter, I'm going to explain why preparation and practice might be the most important Pitch Power of all—certainly the one that's most likely to save you when things don't go as planned.

Let's start with the continuation of my story of my first time pitching on TV.

ORIGIN STORY

After my meeting with Jeff Shimer, I went home to celebrate. Then reality hit: I was going to be on live TV the next day, in front of 20 million people, trying to sell the Smart Mop. *Shit.* What was I going to do? What was I going to say? Bloody hell, what was I going to wear?

At eleven-thirty the next morning, I showed up at the giant HSC complex wearing my khakis and a blue shirt. I had all the stuff I used at the home shows I worked: my blue bucket, a bucket of water, a bottle of ketchup, a cup of sand, a little bit of bleach, a sponge mop, a string mop, two Smart Mops, and a spare mop head. I'm sure I looked like a custodian.

I walked in and said to the first person I saw at a desk, "I'm here. I'm Anthony Sullivan. I'm on at twelve-thirty." He rustled some papers, picked up the phone, and said, "This kid's down here, mops and all. Do you know anything about it? Oh, yeah. Yeah. He's the kid." Jesus! They didn't even know my name. This was back in the day when you had to be a host or a celebrity to be on the air. There were no twenty-four-year-old British kids on the air, period. But there were pictures of Ivana Trump, Jackie Collins, Omar Sharif, and Frankie Avalon—and then there was me! A nobody!

Finally, he said, "Wait here." So I sat. The clock was ticking: 11:35. Eventually, they pointed me back toward the studios, but as I got there a portly, brash man named Dan Dennis, who was the show host, came storming out. I didn't know him, and he certainly didn't know who I was, but he wasn't happy. "What the heck?" he shouted to his assistant, the director, or whoever would listen. "A freaking mop? This is a freaking jewelry show! Cubic zirconia! I don't need to have a mop on the show! I won't make any money today! I don't need some kid who's never been on TV before! Whose fucking idea was this?"

This went on for a while until I was pretty pissed off. I was already a nervous wreck, and I needed someone to come in and say everything was going to be okay, not curse me out of the studio. Finally, Dan went back on the air and the crew calmed things down. "Don't worry about it," they told me. "Dan's just pissed." That sort of thing.

After a few minutes, they walked me into Studio A, and I started to set up on the stage. But as I got my water and filled my buckets, I noticed there was no table. I told one of the crew members I needed one and he said, "We don't have any tables." This was an emergency: I needed something to put my ketchup and sand and mop heads on! Somebody found me a table, but now I was running late. I was sweating. When they put the microphone and earpiece on me, I was completely freaking out. Live TV. Twenty million people. No pressure.

Then, minutes before I was about to go live, this guy named Jim came over and said, "Sir, you can't get the floor wet."

Are you kidding me? I'm about to have a heart attack while I'm standing here, and you're telling me I can't mop the floor? As calmly as I could, I said, "I'm selling a mop, buddy. I'm going to clean the floor. There'll be a clean spot."

"Well, you'll be in trouble.'

"Arrest me," I replied. Then I realized that there was a better way to handle this. "Tell you what," I said, "when I'm done I'll clean the whole studio. I'm good at cleaning floors".

After that, I stopped talking and focused on setting up my joint, just like I would do at a home show or street market. Only I wasn't at a home show. I was in a TV studio with robotic cameras that moved by themselves. There was no cameraman. I'd never seen anything like it. I could see Dan over on another stage. All of a sudden he walked over and stuck out his hand and said, "Hello, Anthony."

"Hello, Dan."'

"How's your day going?"

"Good . . . actually it's a little tough, I don't have all my props, it's my first time . . .

"Good."

Then I realized that the robotic cameras had moved into position. The red light was on!

Shit, we're live.

I felt like an idiot. The only words I could muster were, "Are we on?" Yes, the first thing of any substance that I said on live television was "Are we on?" What a moron! I looked at the camera like it was a firing squad.

Dan turned to the crew and announced, "This is Anthony Sullivan. He's never done this before."

For a moment, I absolutely froze. I went full "deer in the headlights." I didn't know what to do. I was looking at the camera, looking at Dan, and looking at the camera again. Meanwhile, my brain was screaming:

> Don't fuck this up. Just do the pitch. It's the only thing you know right now. The only thing that's going to save you is your pitch. You pitched Jeff yesterday and said you were the guy. You can't do it? Yes, you can. Just go to your pitch.

Practice to the Rescue

At the markets in England and America, when I was ballying a tip and someone was trying to walk past, I'd say, "Sir, what kind of mop do you use?" Nine times out of ten, he'd stop and reply, "I don't mop, my wife does it." Then I've got him, because he's engaged me. So out of pure desperation, I said the only thing I could think of:

"So, Dan, what kind of mop do you use at home?"

Dan replied, "I don't mop the floor."

A layup answer that I'd heard a thousand times from cocky husbands at flea markets! Perfect.

"Well, who cleans the floor in your house?"

"My wife does."

The standard answer; now I'm taking control.

"What kind of mop does she use?"

"I don't know."

"Does she use one of these?" I held up the string mop, then the sponge mop, and then went right into my pitch. I started working Dan like I was at a street market and he was my tip. Because he had been a jerk to me, I decided that I was going to *drill* this guy. I was going to make him beg for my mops. Forget the camera. I was going to sell *Dan.*

I started pitching him and I don't think I looked at the camera the whole time. Now, back in those days Home Shopping Club would put a five-minute clock on the screen in case a product was bombing and they needed to get the host off the air fast. Well, I was pitching and my time was *flying*. Suddenly, just like that, my five minutes were down to thirty seconds!

Before I could react, Dan yelled at someone on the set, "Get that clock off the screen, who put that clock up there?" Then back to me, "Anthony, this is unbelievable—this mop is incredible." It turned out that while I had been fumbling through my first-ever appearance, the phone lines had exploded. I had struck a nerve with the audience at home, who had been falling asleep listening to Dan drone on about cubic zirconia. The sales numbers were screaming.

I kept pitching, and I had Dan completely engaged—"under the ether," as we say in the pitching business. My appearance lasted just twenty-two minutes, but in that time HSC sold all five thousand mops! It was over before I knew it, but I didn't care because time stood still. I had Dan under the ether so it didn't matter to him, either. I probably had all five thousand people at home under the ether, too.

THE PERSUADER!

The Persuader is an experienced superhero, so he knows that even the best go blank from time to time. That's why every pitching hero keeps a store of can't miss, go-to material in his back pocket.

"Even if you haven't practiced your pitch enough to know it by reflex, you can have some basic lines and stories memorized so that if you lose the thread of a job interview or client call, you won't stammer and look silly," the Persuader says. "However, if you can, hedge your bets. In addition to having material I know backwards and forwards, I also take rough notes—even when I'm meeting with someone in person—so I don't lose my train of thought."

I took home a measly $250 that day for my efforts, but couldn't have been happier. I was on my way. I had crushed my first-ever appearance on live TV and we had sold out! If you're in the selling game, you know that selling out is what we aim for. HSC did not have one mop left in inventory. The thing is, I was just trying to save my butt after I froze up. The pitch saved me. If I hadn't been so well prepared, I would have blown my best chance, and I probably wouldn't have the career I have today.

THE REVEAL

This Pitch Power isn't glamorous, but it might be the most important of all. It certainly saved my butt when my nervousness was off the charts and everything was on the line.

OBSESSIVE PREPARATION

Know exactly what you want to say and do before you go into your pitching situation. This obviously applies to selling or presenting, but it also makes sense in scenarios where advance planning might not seem to make as much sense. Before you call your credit card company to pitch for a better rate, know your opening line and talking points. Before you approach the attractive woman at the club, rehearse what you will say if she declines your offer for a drink. Before you head out to shop for a car, practice lines that will help you get the deal you want, like "My wife is picking me up here at three o'clock, so if we haven't done a deal by then, sorry."

Practice is everything, which is why the best way to learn to pitch is to get out and do it. Start practicing somewhere consequence-free, like a bar or club where you can try to meet new people. That might seem fraught with nerves and the potential for embarrassment, but I think you'll agree it's better to get shot down by a cute stranger than to blow an interview for your dream job. Pitching is a skill, and the more you use your Pitch Powers, the smoother and more effortless using them will become. Repetition is the key to reaching that point where you're not thinking, just doing. If you want to persuade people, leave nothing to chance.

Some people worry that too much practice will rob them of any spontaneity. But it's like the difference between watching an improv comedy troupe and the Royal Shakespeare Company doing *Hamlet*. Both are entertainment, but only one is art, and the art takes endless rehearsal. When you've practiced every part of your pitch so much that you do it in your dreams, that *frees* you to improvise and be spontaneous, because if you screw it up you can circle back to what you know.

I never stop practicing my pitches, even today. There's no such thing as too often. A fighter pilot can put a jet down on an aircraft carrier or a Formula One driver can shoot his car around a track at two hundred miles per hour because they have walked that track, flown in the simulator, read the manual, and repeated each step thousands of times. Know what you need to say like you know your own name. Be able to do what you need to do blindfolded. If you're selling cars, you should be able to get into a Ford Escape, turn the radio to SiriusXM, turn on the air conditioning while putting your seat belt on, and text your sales manager that you're taking a customer out for a test drive all while making charming small talk.

Appearing seamless and effortless gives you the aura of an expert, because the customer knows you've done this countless times. I look at it like this: there are already enough obstacles and barriers between you and what you want, from sales resistance to the sheer numbers game of trying to land a new job. Don't put more in your way by fumbling with a product or not knowing an answer that you *should* know.

People love to put themselves in the hands of a skilled expert. Look at Starbucks baristas. Most of those guys can make coffee blindfolded. That's part of the reason you go there: to watch someone pull espresso like an artist while keeping up a friendly patter. The same goes for a great bartender. He knows every ingredient, mixer, glass, and drink formula. He's made any drink you can name a thousand times, so while he's making yours he can keep eye contact with you and carry on a great conversation. Then, before you know it, you drink is done with a flourish, and he's earned a big tip.

Practice . . .

1. . . . what you're going to say. Every great pitchman has a signature line. Billy Mays's signature line for OxiClean was "Powered by the air you breathe, activated by the water you drink." Warms my heart. I use it today as the current OxiClean pitchman. That line takes something that might seem common, a household cleaning product, and makes it relevant and even friendly. But that line came from lots of trial and error.

Your speech should be smooth, confident, and well-paced, and that means practice. Back in my street market days, when I was selling the Amazing Washmatik car washer in places like Croyde Bay in Devon on the English coast, I'd attract a crowd by telling the punters that I was going to "make water run uphill." That always stopped a few people in their tracks. Once I had them gathered around, I'd say, "Imagine giving your car a shower instead of a bath!" and then show them how to do it. By the time I was done, I always had a few people begging me to take their money. If I'd just stuck to the facts—the "features and benefits," as so many sales guys say—I might not have eaten that night.

Your facts are like a British secret agent. He's good looking, with chiseled features and twinkling blue eyes, but he's driving a Toyota Corolla, wearing jeans and a ripped T-shirt, and drinking Budweiser out of a can. Ugh. Put him in a tux, give him a vodka martini (shaken, not stirred, of course), slip him behind the wheel of an Aston Martin, and now you have James Bond. Same man, different presentation. One barely gets a glance; the other won't let you look away. That's the power of a well-rehearsed patter that makes people smile and captures their imagination.

2. . . . what you're going to do. From time to time on HSN, I pitch the H2O Mop X5 steamer. It's a complicated piece of equipment with a lot of parts—wands, heads, you name it—and I've developed the *perfect* pitch for it. Outside of spending about $100,000 to build a set that would make my demonstrations even smoother and more dramatic, I don't think I could make that pitch any better. I would challenge anyone to beat me at that pitch. But one of the reasons it's so good is that I have spent hundreds of hours putting that steamer together, taking it apart, swapping out heads and handles, and manipulating every piece until it's second nature. I'm like a surgeon with the X5. Because of that, I don't have to watch my hands. I can talk to the viewer and tell them how the X5 is going to help them clean their windows, floors, and carpets while I show them how incredibly easy it is to use. I can maintain eye contact the whole time.

Even if your pitch doesn't involve manipulating a product, know how you're going to use your physicality and objects. Are you going to bring printed materials with you, like a resume or samples of work? Where will you keep them and when will you bring them out? If you're attending an audition, how will you cross to your mark and what will you do when you get there? If you're a real estate agent showing a house, do you know how to work the surround sound and programmable thermostat so you can wow a potential buyer?

You should be able to perform whatever physical tasks your pitch requires without pausing in your speech or taking your eyes off the crowd. It should look like magic.

3. . . . what you'll bring. You're blowing them away at your audition. You're the right type, have the right background, your head shots are perfect, and you're charming the pants off the director. Then she asks you to read the prepared dialogue, and you spend half a minute flipping pages to find the scene, muttering, "Just a second . . . this is, no . . . give me one second . . . I know it's—here it is." That's deadly. You just killed all the buzz you'd created because you didn't put a two-cent paper clip on the page you needed.

If it takes you more than three seconds to whip out a pen, business card, or resume, or open up a PowerPoint deck, you're taking too long. Part of preparation means knowing what you're likely to need for your pitch, knowing where it is, and having it at hand so you can produce it effortlessly, like a magician pulling a coin from behind a child's ear. Have a mental checklist—*business cards in shirt pocket, pen in inside coat pocket, resume in briefcase*—and repeat ten times.

4. . . . what you'll wear. Steve Jobs was one of the greatest pitchmen I ever saw, and he wasn't a pitchman at all. He was a legendary innovator, but he also represented something—genius, magic, whatever you want to call it. Part of his presence and pitching prowess was his uniform: jeans, black turtleneck, and white sneakers. He wore the same thing every day, even at his huge national events when he rolled out products like the iPhone. For Billy Mays, it was his blue shirt and khakis.

Plan what you're going to wear just as intentionally. What kind of impression do you want to make? Who's your audience? What's your goal? If you're interviewing at a buttoned-down, white shoe law firm, you're going to wear the best suit you can afford. If you're heading up your advertising agency's pitch to a new client, maybe something more creative. If you're going to be waiting on a table of wealthy society matrons and you want to score a big tip, accent your basic black with a piece of vintage jewelry they're sure to comment on.

Plan your personal presentation as carefully as you plan your pitch: clothing, hair, accessories, everything. Remember,

INCOMPETENT SIDEKICK: THE PROCRASTINATOR

This sidekick can turn even the most promising pitching situation into a shit-show. All he has to do is tempt you to put off preparing or practicing because *Stranger Things* is on, the Broncos are playing the Raiders, or it's a Thursday. You see, the seemingly effortless pitch comes the same way the seemingly effortless golf swing comes: hours and hours of effort. You can't half ass it a half hour before you go into your meeting. Ignore the Procrastinator by calendaring your pitching prep and practice sessions; i.e., "Wednesday, 6:30 p.m., one-hour pitching practice and preparation." Then make like Nike and just do it.

you don't know what small detail will put you over the top—or sink you. Leave nothing to chance.

WITH GREAT POWER COMES GREAT RESPONSIBILITY

You are not the first person to do what you are about to do. That's something most people forget when they confront a pitching scenario, whether it's an audition or a sales meeting. But there is a world of people who have already made the pitch you're going to make and you can learn from them. Remember, according to Pablo Picasso (who allegedly said it), "Good artists create; great artists steal."

Learn to borrow from the best. Read books about pitching or sales. Study people like Billy Mays and Ron Popeil. Go online and watch old spots for classic products. Watch the shopping channels. Read articles about best and worst things to say at a job interview. Find out who's the best in the world at what you're trying to do and steal from them—"butchering," we call that in the pitching world. Billy used to call me the "Butcher of Bayonne." You won't be violating any intellectual property rights. Everyone steals everything in the world of pitching, because the only thing that matters is what works.

Another thing that's essential to prepare is your voice and delivery. Think about it: the one common element to any pitching situation, from waiting tables to buying a car to pitching a potential client, is that you will have to speak. Tone and excitement and intonation and inflection are critical, because different audiences respond to different deliveries. I've had the good fortune to work in a country where people like my English accent, and that's worked for me. Billy Mays found his crazy volume and intensity that people loved. Chris Rock has an intonation that makes you want to listen. Anthony Bourdain sounds sophisticated but knows when to drop an f-bomb. Sportscaster Joe Buck is in a league all by himself, and even a guy like Howard Stern spent years finding his voice.

A great speaking voice and style is not something you are born with; it is something you develop consciously. Barack Obama is an incredible orator, but you know he's worked endlessly on that effortless-looking, cool style. Sarah Palin is the opposite. Her voice and delivery are naturally like nails on a blackboard, but she hasn't made the choice to do something about them. She could work with an elocution coach and develop a speaking style that appeals to people, but she hasn't. People seem to like that she sounds unpolished, like a regular person. Barbara Walters did the opposite: she has a speech impediment, chose to own it, and she's one of the most successful interviewers in history.

Find your volume, your sweet spot. Understand the audience and develop a voice and delivery that's authentic for you but also suits the audience. For example, a motivational speech to a big room will demand a lot more energy than an intimate conversation on a first date. Also, if you have an accent or other natural speech affectation, own it. Own your accent, own your speech impediment, own your style. Own anything that makes you distinct, including your physical look, but be intentional about it.

Be polished, be tailored to the environment, but be *memorable*. Plan on ways you can surprise your audience and stand out from the crowd. Remember, in any situation where you break out your Pitch Powers, you're probably going to be one in a multitude. If your ad agency is pitching a new account, you might be one of a dozen shops doing the same thing. If you're hitting your college professor up for extra credit, you might be one of a hundred students in the same lecture hall. If you're trying to get a better rate on a mortgage, you're one of hundreds of thousands of customers. If you're anonymous, you will get anonymous results. Figure out how you can be surprising, unexpected, and unique. It's more fun for them and for you.

I gave a keynote speech before a big business group in 2015 and everyone was expecting me to talk about pitching or networking. But I don't really have much to add on those subjects. So I got up and said, "I want to talk about relationships. Friendship and business. I do business with people I like. In my business, over the last twenty years, I've developed incredible friendships. If you run a good business, those friendships can last forever and, all of a sudden, you've cultivated this great group of friends who you can depend on through good times and bad."

The audience was barely breathing. I had them under the ether. I went into my Billy Mays story about *The Tonight*

Show. I took it to the obvious ending, Billy's death, and said that the friendships you make in your business will help you endure, and you *will* have catastrophic losses. Whether it's bankruptcy, a lawsuit, a partner who leaves you, or a divorce, you will have losses. Who are you going to depend on? The friendships, your vendors, the people you work with, your colleagues. Those friendships are going to be tried and tested, and that's priceless.

I finished by saying, "I appreciate you wanting to come in tonight and talk about networking, but what you're doing is trying to cultivate friendships. With that, my name is Anthony Sullivan, thank you very much." The audience went nuts. They had expected me to talk about pitching and networking, but I had surprised them, and they were delighted.

Other scenarios where this Pitch Power helps good triumph over evil:

- **A competitive business RFP.** If you're not familiar, RFP is a request for proposal. If you make your living providing services for other businesses, prospective clients will ask you for an RFP if they want you to compete for their business. If you make the first cut, you'll usually be asked for an in-person presentation. Whether your business is advertising or IT, this is where prep and practice can boost your bottom line. Do your background research on the prospect and know their problems. Find out who you're competing with and find their weaknesses. Rehearse your presentation and plan for disaster. What will you do if the AV system tanks and you have no PowerPoint? What will you say if your time gets cut in half?
- **A keynote address.** Public speaking, bigger fear than death, yada, yada. You've heard it. Well, if you'd seen

what I've seen—world-class CEOs and innovators sweating and shaking like heroin addicts at the prospect of addressing an audience for five minutes—you'd know it's true. So know this: if you're not a natural or experienced speaker, you *will* panic and go blank when it's just you, the mic, and five hundred people. What will save you is preparation. Memorize your speech. Have some cue cards to use as life preservers if you start to sink, but memorize your speech. Know it backwards and forwards. When your heart is hammering, you'll automatically, instinctively start running through your points. Trust me. Eventually, you'll realize that lightning hasn't struck and that you're actually *doing* it.

- **Extensive traveling.** Traveling? Yeah. Here's why. If you've ever taken a multi-week, multi-city, or multi-country trip, you know not everything goes as planned. At some point, maybe multiple times, there's going to be a lost hotel reservation, a canceled flight, an unavailable rental car, something. When something goes pear-shaped, you're going to have to persuade a clerk or customer service rep to help you out. In other words, you're going to pitch, and you'll get better results if you're prepared. Know your legal rights as a traveler. Know the other hotels in the same class in the cities you're going to. Know your credit card company's policies. Plan what you'll say to gate agents and concierges, always remembering that a smile gets you more than a scowl.

Story-Furthering Interlude

If there's a person in the pitching and sales world who has benefited from the power of practice and preparation, it would be hard to top Joy Mangano. Today, she's the president of

Ingenious Designs, LLC, an HSN icon, holder of more than a hundred patents, and the subject of a major Hollywood biopic, *Joy*, starring Academy Award winner Jennifer Lawrence. But she started out in 1990 designing her first product, the Miracle Mop, and when she appeared on QVC to pitch it she sold eighteen thousand units in thirty minutes and a star was born. Her secrets? Planning and preparation.

"Planning is an understatement," Joy says. "You have to live it! I never put a product in front of my consumer unless it is part of me, and that can take years of dreaming and planning and hard work. It's not hard to know why I fell in love with a product I created. But you have to be able to find those perfect words that convey your product love with the original energy and enthusiasm that led you to create it in the first place. That's lots of thinking, and planning, and using the product, and talking about it with everyone around you!"

Joy also shares some advice that might seem unusual but that's really quite smart. "Early in my career, I prepared for a product to sell slowly, and what to do if that happens, but I never prepared for the consumers to fall in love and for it to sell out like wildfire," she concludes. "So I learned, you have to prepare for the worst AND the best, and be ready for even your wildest dreams to come true!"

Plot Twist!

One thing you can never be completely prepared for is anger. When I was selling at British street markets, it wasn't uncommon for someone who didn't like the product I'd just sold them to come back while I was pitching a later audience and stand at the edge of the crowd, glowering at me. Sometimes, they would be holding the mop or car washer or whatever that I'd sold them earlier or the previous weekend, and sometimes they would be disruptive. Occasionally, someone would try to pollute my joint by saying something like "You sold me this last week and it's a piece of shit. I want my ten quid back!"

When you're in sales, you're going to have unhappy customers. What can throw you is when you strike a nerve in another type of pitch: when you say the wrong thing at a job interview, for instance, or when someone you're waiting on lashes out at you. If and when that happens, here are a few things I suggest:

1. **Keep your cool.** There's nothing to be gained by snapping back at the other person. Think about it like this: it's your job to keep the amount of overall angst in the room at a consistent level. The more upset the other guy gets, the calmer you should become.
2. **Know the reason.** People generally don't lash out irrationally for no reason. Maybe the lady shouting at you had a really terrible day. Maybe the guy on the other end of the phone has been sick with the flu for a week and hasn't slept. Nobody's trying to make your day bad on purpose. Remember that and you're more likely to get an apology than more rage.
3. **Consider your audience.** Sometimes, the angry person isn't alone. I've had people call up when I've been on HSN and tell me they thought the product I was pitching was crap. If I lose my cool at them, 90 million people might watch me do it. So I have to smile and try to help the caller solve her problem, even if she's rude. At a meeting, a hotel desk, or a restaurant, other people are watching and they're going to judge how professional and skilled you are based on how you handle an angry jerk.

WHAT WOULD BILLY DO?

Billy Mays here! You don't want to prepare for your pitch? You must love failure! Let me tell you, I prepared like nobody else. I would rehearse and rehearse and that gave me the freedom to improvise great lines while I was on TV pitching a product live. So here's what you do: Practice your pitch from beginning to end. Anticipate the three toughest questions you're likely to hear, and practice your responses to those. Practice your awesome close and "wow" offer, the one the other person won't be able to refuse. And then when you're sick of practicing them, practice one more time!

When I had an angry punter at the public markets, I used that to my advantage. I always asked them to wait until I was done with my pitch and if they did, I would refund their money plus £1, no questions asked. Most of the time, they agreed, and I handed them their money in full view of everyone. It made me look like a good guy and removed any dark clouds of doubt my unhappy customer might've cast over me.

Training Montage

The more hours you put in, the better you will get, and the more real you can make your practice situation, the better it will be. You don't learn to play soccer by kicking balls into a net. You put on your cleats, go down to the stadium when there's nobody there, and play in the arena, if you can do it. Get yourself as close to the action as possible.

This can involve some strange things. Years ago, I was pitching a vegetable slicer in England and I needed to have my pitch down in a very short time. So I set up a fake joint in my backyard garden, complete with a fake vegetable slicer, all my vegetables lined up, a table, and a "gozinta"—a hole that all the waste and trash "goes into." I would be back there for hours talking to an imaginary audience and going through every stage of my pitch. My roommates genuinely thought I had lost my shit. They couldn't understand why I was standing out in the drizzle, talking to an imaginary audience. But nobody was watching me, and I knew I was not ready to go out and pitch this product. There was no way I was going to get up in front of a lot of people with the product and fumble through the demos and not be fluid.

Plus, the blade was sharp and I didn't want to cut my fingers off. So there was that.

When I finally did go onto my joint with the slicer, I killed it. I sold out. Another old joke was that the slicer was so sharp and could slice veggies so thin that I had gone through the entire summer using only one cucumber in my kitchen. It was hilarious.

But that's what pitching takes. If you really want to be brilliant at pitching and persuasion, you have to pay the same price you pay to be great at playing the piano, sinking jump shots, or writing: putting in an extraordinary amount of practice. You will drive people crazy. Your friends and family will think you've gone slightly mad. If you speak to my friends and family members from back in the day, they had no idea what I was doing.

If you can find a good friend who feels like giving everything to your cause, ask them if they'll help you out and watch your pitch. Get some feedback. Also, we live in an age when everyone has a video camera, so record yourself. I never had that luxury, but you do. You'll hate watching yourself at first and think you look and sound like a complete tool, but you'll pick up areas where you can have more energy or better detail.

Finally, don't mistake practice for the real thing. Practice will help you have something to fall back on when you stand in front of your audience and your heart is pounding and your palms are sweating, but it won't stop those things from happening. The first time I ever pitched the car washer at a street market, I was so nervous that I was sure I would faint. But I did the pitch as I'd been taught—and it worked! People gave me money! It was amazing. But assume you're going to be nervous your first time, maybe your first few times. It's normal. My friends who've been in the Marine Corps have told me that while they train and drill you under combat conditions and with all the gear, no amount of training can ever prepare you for being in real combat against people who are trying to kill you. It's something you just have to do and survive.

This isn't combat. This is pitching. You can do it. Prepare, and you'll survive.

SCENARIOS FOR USING THE "OBSESSIVE PREPARATION" PITCH POWER

Q: *You prepared and prepared for the meeting and then it turns out you got the days mixed up. You're prepared for the wrong meeting! How will you get out of this scrape?*

A: You won't. In a pitching situation, being disingenuous will sink you, and anyone with half a brain will know if you're BSing your way through a pitch you're not ready for. Make up an excuse and reschedule. Then prepare to dazzle them.

Q: *Word gets back to the company you're interviewing with that you were asking questions and prying into their history. How do you respond?*

A: Be direct: you're trying to learn as much about them as possible so you can ask smart questions and suggest great ideas—and because you want an edge over the other candidates. People love that competitive fire.

Q: *You get five friends to give you feedback on your speech and they all say it stinks. Do you rewrite it, ignore them, or something in between?*

A: One opinion is just that, an opinion. The same opinion twice is a pattern. The same opinion three times is a consensus. If five pals say your pitch is terrible, tear it up and go back to the drawing board.

POWER NUMBER FOUR

MAKE AN ENTRANCE AND TAKE CONTROL

Good for saving the day in debates, stage performances, speeches, client presentations.

WHEN WE LAST LEFT OUR HERO . . .

You were up to your eyebrows in note cards and Google searches, figuring out what to say, how to say it, and how to show up for your big pitch. But that's it for the prep work. Now we start talking about how to pitch when you're standing (or sitting) in front of someone who could, maybe, change your life.

ORIGIN STORY

I'd always known the power of making an entrance and commanding everyone's attention with word pictures, gestures, and energy. That's how we survived in the tough street markets of London and Wales. The reality is that nobody wants to be sold, but everybody wants to be *spellbound*. But I never understood how completely one person could take control, not just of a studio, but of an audience of millions until I saw Billy Mays do it on HSN.

It was 1995 and Billy was both a friend and a rival. I had been pitching products on the network and making a nice name for myself, so I wasn't happy when I saw him come around the corner in the back hallways of HSN, charging ahead like a bull and grinning his thousand-watt grin. Turned out that the inventors of a carpet-cleaning product called Zap Off needed a pitchman to sell it, and they'd found Billy Mays. *Shit*. If the folks at HSN thought I was good, wait until they saw Billy in action.

Of course, since Billy was barging his way onto my turf in my town, I didn't do anything to help him get acclimated at HSN. In fact, I did my best to sabotage him. The day he was going live, I stuck my head into the studio and saw him on his hands and knees on the set, sweating and nervous and trying to figure out how he was going to demo the product. Then, because this is just what friends do, I made him even more self-conscious by walking into the studio just before he went live. I did that because I knew it would drive him crazy.

I know how hard it is to create an effective pitch for a product that you're selling for the first time on live television; I've done it and it's one of the hardest things I've ever attempted. While there are tried-and-true pitching principles that we always use, coming up with a successful pitch involves a lot of trial and error, and HSN isn't the place for that. After all, the network has that computer screen that displays live sales stats and can instantly show a host whether they're killing it or bombing. If you're going to make it on HSN, you need to get results.

But for Billy, ignorance was bliss: he didn't know anything about the screen, which was good because it would've made him even more nervous. I thought about pointing it out to him, but even I'm not *that* sadistic.

Before he went on, we chatted in the greenroom. I told him his pitch seemed scattered and he gave me his patented "that was harder than it looks" glance. Then I settled into the chewed-up, coffee-stained blue couch and watched Billy walk onto the set in front of millions of viewers—and grow wings.

He tore into a pitch that was a combination of one-liners from the road and new stuff he came up with on the fly, in the moment. It was incredible to watch. He dominated the set with his physical presence from the moment he walked on. He invented the tagline "Just aim, spray, and walk away" on the spot, and the company still uses it today, more than twenty years later. He improvised more lines that it would take a marketing team weeks to come up with, including "I used to have a dog named Spot, now I don't" and "If you've got a golden reliever—I mean golden retriever." His pitching instincts were on full display and dialed up to eleven.

But the most amazing thing was that nobody could look away from Billy. He stood low in his pitching stance like a quarterback about to take a snap, beads of sweat running down his forehead, his voice booming so powerfully that he almost overloaded the microphones. He found his one-shot camera, and started to work right to the viewer and do what he did best: mesmerize. The hosts were completely irrelevant. Billy commanded the attention of every person watching, whether they were watching live in Florida or in homes around the country.

It was the making of a pitching superstar. Rival though I was, I couldn't help but be impressed. The phone lines exploded. The graph that shows the number of calls went up and up until the tips of the bars started turning red. Hurricane

THE PERSUADER!

Every superhero benefits from the element of surprise, and the Persuader is no different. When I confront a difficult pitch, I try to seize the advantage by making an entrance that nobody expects. Sometimes that involves entering the situation with great confidence, like *I'm* the one who belongs there, not the other person: I'll walk on a car lot and call a salesman over to tell him exactly what I'm looking for. Other times it means being disarming: I'll go up to a harried airline service agent at an airport and immediately compliment her on her outfit or smile. The idea is to take control by forcing the other person off his or her script. That way, I determine what happens next.

Billy had made landfall at HSN. Neither he nor the company would ever be the same.

THE REVEAL

What Billy Mays did that day at HSN was demonstrate his world-class skill with an important Pitch Power:

MAKE AN ENTRANCE AND TAKE CONTROL

Assume that 90 percent of the people who walk into the same pitching situation as you are going to do so meekly, apologetically, and haltingly. They're going to be afraid to stand out and unwilling to seize control of the moment and own the room. That's not what a pitching superhero does. If you watch a professional pitchman, he takes charge of the situation with boldness and confidence. He doesn't wait for the audience to set the tone; he captures everyone's attention by being charismatic, creative, and positive.

How do you make an entrance and take control of a situation where you're clearly the one who wants something? Doesn't that put the other person—the one with the power to say no—in the position of power? Only if you think of it that way. When I teach people about pitching, one of the first pieces of advice I offer is that you have to love your product, especially if your product is *you*. See what you're offering as precious and desirable, whether it's your time, your expertise, or your business. The other party—whether it's a recruiter, customer, or someone you're hitting on—should be so *lucky* to be the one *you* choose. That's the attitude of the pitching superhero, a sort of "fake it 'til you make it" confidence.

If I make my entrance with that kind of vibe, I'm going to ask you a question to which I already know the answer. I might make some outlandish statement that I will then substantiate. I might offer you something or propose a deal that sounds too good to be true. By doing those things right off the bat, I dictate what's going to happen in the next five minutes. You're not in control, even though I let you think you are. *I am.*

Anatomy of a Superpower

Think about sales resistance not as a wall or barrier but as something like those Plexiglas riot shields that police use. When you encounter someone you don't know who you think wants to persuade you to do something you don't want to do, you raise your shield. Now, think about being someone who's hearing pitches from a lot of strangers in succession: a director holding auditions, a woman from HR interviewing job candidates, an attractive woman sitting alone at a cafe. Each time he or she meets someone new, the shield goes up. As the new person becomes more familiar and everybody becomes more comfortable, the shield drops.

Each time someone new walks into the room, the interviewer or director or whoever needs to lift that shield all over again—and that sucker is heavy. People would rather not feel the need to put up their sales resistance all the time, because it's hard work. Making an entrance, taking control, and getting the other person to feel instantly comfortable is all about giving him or her an excuse not to raise that heavy shield.

THREE TYPES OF SALES RESISTANCE

Psychology says there are three types of resistance that come into play when people find themselves in a sales situation:

1. **Reactance.** They object to the sales process itself, the idea of *being* sold at all.
2. **Skepticism.** They view you and your claims with suspicion, pretty sure that you're throwing them a line of pure bullshit.
3. **Inertia.** They fear change and don't want to commit to anything, even something that will benefit them.

Pitch Powers are designed to get you past all three kinds of resistance, and making an entrance and taking control is where that begins. By being funny and charming ("Hello, handsome!") you make people forget about it being a sales situation. By being specific about your claims, you bypass their natural skepticism. By being the solution to their problems—showing an interviewer how valuable you could be by sharing information about his company that even *he* didn't know, for example—you make your solution so compelling that it breaks through their inertia.

Say we have an enterprising waitress with a table of six cynical salesmen to wait on. These guys fancy themselves to be true hard-asses who've seen it all, heard it all, and sold it all. There's no pitch they haven't tried, and they're expecting to be sold by a waitress trying to inflate their bill and her tip. But our pitch-savvy server decides that for these world-weary road warriors, she's going to take control of the situation.

She greets and seats them, but when they tell her they're ready to order, she says, "No. I'm not going to take your order."

What? This gets their attention and gets past their reactance. *One barrier down.* They look around at each other. *Not going to take their order?* She continues, "I can see you gentlemen are tired at the end of a long business trip, right? Well, here's what I want you to do. I want you to trust me. Let me surprise you with an order of our manager's choosing, including cocktails. If you don't love what I bring, it's on the house. What do you say?"

By giving them a novel experience, this smart young woman has these gents smiling and nodding and has obliterated their skepticism. *Two barriers down.* Their fear that she'll bring them the most expensive food and liquor on the menu is overcome by their delight and curiosity at such an unusual offer. *Final barrier down.* They agree and she disappears into the kitchen. Of course, she never speaks to the manager; she's served guys like this a thousand times and knows exactly what they'll like: a little filet, a little seafood, some appetizers, a lot of it off-menu stuff that most patrons don't even know about.

What makes this a perfect pitching example is that the waitress keeps making entrances. Every time she comes back with a different course or a new cocktail to try, she has the chance to surprise and dazzle, so she does. She pairs food with unique cocktails and matches everything with funny patter. But here's the key: the bill is quite reasonable. She hasn't gouged her customers, which is what they expected. Now she's given them two delightful surprises: the dining experience, and then the check.

Now these salesmen have no sales resistance left. They've been taken care of, and even more than the food, they love that their server took control of their experience so they didn't have to do any work. But she saves the coup de grâce for the end: she asks them if they would like dessert and an after-dinner drink. Feeling cared for, celebratory, and generous, they order desserts and a bottle of Macallan 18 scotch, which, with this restaurant's markup, runs about $400. The final tab is about $1,200, and our merry band, feeling they've had one of the best dining experiences of their lives, tips our waitress a cool $300. Not bad for three hours of work.

If you want to take control of any situation as soon as you walk in the room, and get what you want, try using these three next-level skills:

1. Create "sell lines." This is the pitch, the patter, the spiel. I had a host of money lines with the Amazing Washmatik (the car washer I pitched in the UK), like "The faster you go, the faster it flows," "As soon as you stop, it stops," and "It's like giving your car a shower instead of a bath." Those are good lines, lines that paint pictures.

The waitress's sell line was her refusal to take the salesmen's order and her command for them to trust her. Whatever you're trying to pitch and whoever you're trying to pitch it to, come up with your own poetry—lines that make whatever you're trying to pitch unforgettable. In a job interview, if you're trying to highlight your dedication, you might try saying, "While you're home sleeping, I'll be here working. I'm overtime, all the time."

A great sell line does three things: it communicates the value you offer, does it in a way that conveys total confidence, and surprises the listener so much that they stop in their tracks. What can you say in a pitching situation that will do that? I'll tell you right now: it's got nothing to do with features and benefits, prices, discounts, or any of that other rubbish. Your job is to intrigue, shock, and fascinate.

By the way, one of the best sell lines in any situation is to flat-out tell your listener that you don't care about the result. You don't need the sale; you just want to give the customer the honest information nobody else is giving them. You don't care if you get the girl's number; you just want to enjoy her company. You don't care if you get the part or not; you just want to give the director something he's never seen.

2. Appeal to greed. One quick way to get people's instant buy-in is to appeal to their self-interest. Offer them something free, even if it's cheap, or promise them extraordinary value. Timeshare companies go the first way by offering you a free weekend at a resort in return for you sitting through one of those high-pressure, daylong sell-a-thons. They bribe you into putting yourself in a sales situation where you wouldn't normally be caught dead.

Could you use this in a work situation? Absolutely. Appealing to self-interest always works. For example, an employee at my production company wanted to ask me for a bigger bonus.

Fine. I don't have a problem with that. But she came into my office and the first words out of her mouth were "Boss, did I do anything wrong this year? My bonus was only $7,000." Immediately, I was on the defensive. There were so many better ways she could have handled the situation.

She could have come in and said, "You know, I love working here. You're a great boss, and I really enjoy my job. So I'm really afraid to ask you this, but I'm struggling financially and I'd love to make more money. But I don't want to just make more money. I have some ideas on how to save the company money, so we can grow and everybody can make more. Would you like to hear them?" I'm not going to say no to that! Then maybe she'd say, "If we did this and this, I think I could save you 10 percent a year. If I could do that, do you think maybe we could talk about a raise? I'm a single mom and I'd really appreciate it."

I would have said, "Come in on Monday, sit down and detail exactly what you'll do. If it looks good to me, then do it. Report back to me in two months with the savings, and if you hit your goals, you've got your raise." That's taking control of the situation not only by appealing to my self-interest, but by being positive and honest. It's pitching, not bitching.

3. Engage the senses. When you're starting your pitch, your audience is going to have only two senses engaged: sight and hearing. The more senses you can engage, the better. When you engage a sense, you break through a barrier separating you from your audience. If you have an opportunity to engage someone in a physical manner that's appropriate, do it. In a job interview, that might be your handshake. If you're trying to meet someone new, maybe it's your cologne or perfume, or the light touch of a finger on a forearm at the right time. *Feel this, smell this.* For a waitress, it might be "We've got samples today, would you like a free taste?" Yogurt shops do it all the time. Some restaurants give out free appetizers, compliments of the chef.

Our superhero server engaged her customers' senses by offering them unique drinks and treats that they hadn't had before with zero risk; if they hated them, they didn't pay for them. Taste, smell, mouth feel: all five senses were involved. By the end of the meal, she had them right where she wanted them—and had her tip.

But in making an entrance and taking control, nothing is more important than confidence. You have to assert with total belief that whatever you bring to the room that day is so incredible that your audience won't be able to resist. But don't be too pushy or too soft. The goal is a comfortable conversation where you are in control. Where, even if you're interrupted, you can say, "Let me finish," and the listener submits because he or she is under your spell.

Sometimes, this just means walking into the room as though you're the best thing that's ever been in it. Not in an arrogant way, but with an attitude of "I've found something so wonderful and I have to share it with you!" I've had people come to me looking for their dream job, and I know when it's a good interview because the candidate starts to talk and I think, *You're pitching me on why I should hire you.* You're making it impossible for me not to want to hire you. You can't be timid. You can't be afraid. You have to sell yourself so I see you as indispensable.

In the end, your goal is to make the other person practically beg to give you what you want. State your case with an "Of

INCOMPETENT SIDEKICK: CAPTAIN CRINGE

Captain Cringe is a wimp who can't help but enter a room apologetically, expecting to fail. He instantly sucks the air out of every space he's in, and in the face of even the slightest objections or tough questions, he waves the white flag. Don't let him anywhere near your pitching situation, because even if you have the best features, benefits, or qualifications in the room, he'll crush your chances with his mealymouthed, simpering ways.

course you're going to give me the outcome I want, duh!" confidence, drop the mic, and walk away with a handshake.

WITH GREAT POWER COMES GREAT RESPONSIBILITY

When you're taking control of the encounter, you will start to see your audience's defenses come down. Their body language will change. They'll get comfortable because they've stopped being afraid that you're going to make them do something that's bad for them, like spending money on something they don't want. You'll see them nodding. You're going to see the twinkle in somebody's eye. They might even start sharing information or stories that are supposed to be confidential. Now you're a co-conspirator.

At this point, tone it down. Don't get flashy. Don't *close*. This is not the time for that because you're probably only a few minutes into your encounter. Give the situation space to breathe. You just walked into the big boss's office and blew his socks off. There's a time to stop pitching, and you'll learn to recognize it.

Other essentials of this Pitch Power:

- **Make your entrance strong.** When I talk about making an entrance, I'm not necessarily talking about bursting into the room like you're in a Las Vegas stage show. For one thing, an entrance isn't always about a physical space (though to be fair, 90 percent of the time, it is). If you're pitching a loan officer or credit card company, your "entrance" will be the first things you say on the phone call. However, for now, let's assume you're coming into a space, whether it's a conference room for a client pitch, a car lot showroom, or an office for your annual performance review.

  The strong entrance is a matter of three factors: *pause*, *acknowledgment,* and *preamble*. The *pause* is all about taking a second to get the lay of the land in an unfamiliar space. Where is the person or people you're going to be pitching? Where's the light? Is there a choice of seats? Is there water? You're assessing the pitch environment in two seconds. *Acknowledgment* is all about recognizing people. Stop and thank the receptionist who brought you in, introduce yourself to other people in the room, and even compliment the people who made you feel welcome outside. This is about making yourself memorable and being generous to everyone.

  Finally, the *preamble*. This can be when you make some power moves. Cross to the table, desk, or whatever and boldly shake the hands of everyone you're pitching, introduce yourself, and tell them how great it is to be there and how you think you can be the answer to their prayers (or something to that effect). But the preamble doesn't always end there. Is there a chair available at the head of the table? Take it. Total power move. I love to do that because (a) nobody has the balls to do it, and (b) it ensures that everyone will be looking at me when I speak. Also, if there's bottled water, before you sit, grab yourself one without being asked and ask everybody else if they want one. Obviously, you're doing these things sweetly and even self-deprecatingly ("Anybody mind if I sit at the end? Dad always did it at home and I've always wondered what it felt like"), but you're making the space your own. Try it.

- **No overt power plays.** I've just given you some small power plays to try, but that's it. Do not try to alpha your audience. No crushing handshakes, no being the last person to sit down, none of that crap. You'll just waste people's time and look like a douche.
- **Don't use fear.** When you're making the case that you're the solution to someone's problem, trying to scare them makes you look manipulative, and people hate to be manipulated. Fear doesn't work. For instance, after years of pitching products, I can tell you that prevention doesn't sell. Try selling a smoke detector to somebody based on the idea of keeping their family from dying in a fire; it's almost impossible. Why do you think people who sell smoke detectors and home security systems talk about how much you can save on your homeowner's insurance? Because people are motivated by greed, not by something that *might* happen. That's the same reason people only buy life insurance after somebody they know dies.

Other scenarios where this Pitch Power can be the difference between success and failure:

- **Blind dates.** Making an entrance and taking control aren't just useful for quickly impressing someone you're meeting for the first time. That's lovely if he or she is someone you want to spend time with, but what if the match is a mismatch? Well, by clearly and boldly communicating who you are and what you're about, you also find out quickly if the two of you are compatible. Better that than wasting an evening, or several evenings, right?
- **Customer service.** If you're stuck with the job of soothing an unhappy customer or making a bad situation right, there's nothing worse than having to sit and listen to someone bitch for twenty minutes. It wastes everyone's time and accomplishes nothing. Use these pitching techniques to take control and get the conversation going in the right direction and toward a quick resolution, which is what everybody wants.
- **Teaching.** Running a classroom is one of the hardest jobs there is, and good teachers have my highest respect. Make the job a bit easier by using these methods to catch students by surprise and have them hanging on your every word. Tricks like power words and power gestures (which I'll cover below) work wonders in grabbing kids' attention and getting them to shut up, listen, and learn.

Plot Twist!

You're meeting with a small group of angel investors about funding your small start-up company and you want to impress them. You have your entrance choreographed: rather than walk in, awkwardly set up your PowerPoint presentation, and then stumble through it like so many entrepreneurs do, you're going to walk up to each of the partners and hand each one a prototype of your product. Then you're going to step back, deliver a concise monologue on why what you've invented is so wonderful, and then go into the facts and figures.

Sounds great . . . until you get into the room, reach into your messenger bag and to your horror, realize that in your haste you forgot your prototypes! How do you deal with the plot twist of blowing your entrance?

One thing you don't do is cover and pretend everything's all right. You admit your mistake and then move on. You don't keep apologizing for it, either. The truth is that many people, from employers to investors to customers, will judge you more on how you recover from an error than they will on what you do when everything's fine. Blowing your entrance doesn't mean the play's over; you still have lines to deliver and you can still put in one hell of a performance, even earn a standing ovation. Get on with it.

One quick note: don't become dependent on PowerPoint. It's a useful tool, but it's not a substitute for knowing how to pitch.

Training Montage

In the movie *Jerry Maguire*, there's a brief scene that's stuck with me for years. The screen flashes to a smiling older guy in an office with a nameplate on his desk that reads DICKY FOX. He's Jerry's mentor. He says, "I love mornings! I clap my hands every morning and say, 'This is gonna be a great day!'" I do the same thing every morning.

That's the kind of attitude you need if you're going to own the room and take control. Let me tell you what I've done for

WHAT WOULD BILLY DO?

Billy Mays here! When I was pitching anything, I would take control of the situation by using power words and power gestures. "Listen." "Look." "Watch this." "I gotta show you somethin'." "Let me tell you somethin'." "Look at that—unbelievable!" There's amazing power in telling someone, "Stop. Listen." You're commanding them! Then you use your hands: holding them up, raising one finger to make a point, conducting your audience's attention like you're conducting an orchestra. During this, you're constantly appealing to the listener to pay attention and inviting them to be in awe: "Isn't that incredible?" Power words. Power gestures. They're power tools in any pitchman's arsenal, and not just for selling.

years: when I go around town, whether I'm at home in St. Petersburg or on the road, I greet everyone I meet and try to say something complimentary to them. I'll do it with baristas at my favorite coffee place, the waiters at my regular breakfast restaurant, my cleaning lady, you name it. I make a conscious effort to bring some positive energy to everyone whose path crosses mine, and by now it's a habit. It doesn't take any effort, but it sets a tone. It sets me up for success. That positive energy builds and people respond.

People love to feel good. There's this guy named Chris Ullman who in his career has been director of communications at the US Office of Management and Budget, public affairs director for the US Securities and Exchange Commission, and director of communications for the US House of Representatives Budget Committee. But you know what this guy is best known for? Being the four-time national and international whistling champion. That's right. Despite all his accomplishments, what's gotten Ullman on the stage at B.B. King's, on *The Tonight Show,* and performing for the likes of Newt Gingrich, Dick Cheney, and George W. Bush is his world-class skill at whistling. Why? Because there's nothing about whistling that's not happy and cheerful! Even heads of state love to feel good and positive.

If you want to develop this Pitch Power, work on getting up and saying, "Today is going to be a beautiful day. It's not going to rain today. I'm going to spread happiness." If you walk around with your head down, how are you going to be ready to persuade anyone? You need to be a shining light in the room. When you walk into the room, you want people to say, "I want what that guy's having." We all know people like that, who make it feel like wherever they are is the only place worth being. Try to get in the habit of putting out positive energy all day, because it will come back to you.

That's *magnetism*. Here's how I know it works: most of the pitchmen I know have really good-looking girlfriends. They punch way above their weight, because most of them are very average-looking guys. But they make people laugh. They're charming. They're *attractive*, meaning their personality attracts people to them. If you have that quality, you will punch above your weight because people will want to be around you.

Everything else in this chapter is really mechanics, from power words and gestures to pausing to take stock of the room. You can practice them all and become more persuasive. But positivity needs to become part of who you are. The best way to practice this is to put the book down, get in your car, go somewhere public, and try this. Try being a beacon of positive energy—complimenting servers and cashiers, talking about how great a business is, talking about how terrific the day is—and see what kind of results you get from other people. Then try being walled off and standoffish and notice the difference.

If I was selling you, this is where I'd be offering you a guarantee. Because this works. Every time. If you fill up every place you go with positive energy, you will be so excited to get to the next chapter that you won't be able to contain yourself.

SCENARIOS FOR USING THE "MAKE AN ENTRANCE AND TAKE CONTROL" PITCH POWER

Q: *You try some alpha dog moves in a meeting and get serious pushback from someone who considers himself or herself the alpha dog. Back off or try to exert more control?*

A: Back off the obvious power moves, but remember that there's more than one way to take control of a situation. If someone is being aggressive, it's usually because he or she is hiding a lack of preparation or knowledge. So relax and instead, be the one who's hyper-knowledgeable, super prepared or makes everybody laugh.

Q: *You're feeling awful when you face a pitching situation. Maybe you're sick, or maybe you've just had a horrible week. Fake positivity and risk people seeing right through you, admit that you're having a rough go, or postpone?*

A: Postponing is risky because you might not get another shot, but if you're really sick, say so and reschedule. If it's been a rough week, suck it up and get the room laughing. Never, ever complain that you feel tired or that it's been a tough week; it looks like you're making excuses. Once you're on your joint, you'll feel better.

Q: *You're smart enough to know that assistants make the world go 'round, so you want to compliment the assistant of a key client. But you're worried that he/she will think you're hitting on him/her. How do you handle this perilous situation?*

A: Make it about what the other person does, not how she or he looks. "I just wanted to tell you how much I appreciate how professional you are about returning my calls and scheduling meetings. It really makes my work a lot easier." That will always go over well, and a small token of appreciation like a gift card can't hurt, either.

POWER NUMBER FIVE

BREACH THE FORCE FIELD

Good for saving the day in breaking the ice with that cute stranger, trying to meet someone intimidating or famous, selling to people in a public place.

WHEN WE LAST LEFT OUR HERO . . .

You were busy working on your power words and power gestures and practicing how to get everyone's eyes locked on you when you enter a room, without it looking theatrical or having everybody think you're a tool. But what do you do when you have their attention?

ORIGIN STORY

I did the New York City Marathon back in 2010 and there must have been 2 million people on the streets. The spectator support was overwhelming. If you put your name on a piece of duct tape, you would hear it shouted at you at least a thousand times. People were handing out food: bananas, popsicles, jelly beans, raisins, pizza. It was awesome.

Fast-forward to a year ago. The St. Anthony's Triathlon was happening in St. Petersburg, and the run course went right past my house. I'm friends with a lot of triathletes, including Mark Bowstead from New Zealand and Alicia Kaye, and since I wanted to encourage them, and because I was going to have four thousand competitors running past my house, I decided to put up some OxiClean signage along with signs that read GO BO! and GO ALICIA!

After a few minutes, I had an inspiration. I remembered how great the food from the spectators had been when I was doing the New York City Marathon. I also thought about soccer. If you ever played soccer as a kid, your coaches and parents probably gave you orange slices at halftime. Remember how refreshing they were? I doubt there's anybody who doesn't like oranges; they're the universal fruit. Because I've done a few triathlons, I knew how much the runners would be suffering by the time they got to the turn in my street. They'd be overheated, exhausted, and running short on energy. I ran inside my house, got all the oranges I had in the fridge, and started slicing them up.

I didn't have enough to feed four thousand people, but it was amazing how many slices I got. I put them all on ice along with some cantaloupe and took the whole batch out to the front. My mum and her husband, Alan, were in town from England, and they watched. My neighbors, the Shamrocks, looked on while we tried to hand the runners orange and cantaloupe slices as they went by. But strangely, maybe one in twenty actually took them.

At first, I thought that maybe it was because they didn't know if the fruit had been handled in a sanitary way, which I could understand. You wouldn't want to grab an orange slice and then three hours later be retching your guts out because of *E. coli*. So I put the orange slices on cocktail toothpicks and plastic forks, and still, hardly anyone accepted our free, cold oranges.

Then it hit me. This wasn't New York. These men and women weren't running through busy Manhattan streets where people handing out food was all part of the experience. They had been swimming, biking, and running all over the Tampa Bay area, and suddenly here was this grinning pillock in his khakis and blue shirt, handing out fruit. I wasn't an official aid station. I must have seemed downright mad.

I knew then that it was the force field at work. If I was going to help these runners with my cold, juicy oranges, I was going to have to break through.

The Force Field

When you walk into a retail store and a clerk greets you and asks you, "Hi, can I help you find something?" how often do you say, "No, thanks" without even thinking? About 90 percent of the time, I'll bet. You don't want to be helped. Even if you do want to be helped, you want to be helped on your terms. "Can I help you?" is actually a really bad question, because it activates what I call the *force field*.

The force field is the attitude many people maintain that keeps other people at a distance. It's our natural sales resistance and suspicion of ulterior motives, real or imagined. It's our protection against being sold to, coerced, or having something done to us against our will. It's what keeps us from talking to the person next to us on the plane and has us with our heads down, staring at our smartphones, for hours rather than engage with the people around us. *Engaging is scary*, our brains tell us, *but behind the force field, I'm safe.* So we put out that "leave me alone" vibe, and people leave us alone.

Some people have their guard up all the time, even in the middle of a triathlon. I could see it as clear as day: the runners saw me in my OxiClean gear and reacted unconsciously: *He's giving away free oranges, he probably wants my email address or phone number, he wants me to buy OxiClean.* So they kept their distance. Of course, I didn't want anything like that; I just wanted to help, no strings attached. Somehow, I had to get through their force field and earn their trust.

First, I fell back on my county fair pitchman skills. I started shouting, "Free oranges, if you want an orange, slice of orange!" My mum did the same, but nobody cared. Then, because repetition and alliteration are critical in a good street pitch, I changed to "Nice cold, ice cold oranges! Vitamin C, ice cold oranges, get the refreshment!" A few people looked and took slices, but eight out of ten were still passing us by without a glance. My amazing pitching skills were falling flat. Then I thought, *I'm literally at a distance from these athletes. I need to close the distance.* To get the take, I needed to make their problem—pain, heat, fatigue—my problem, too, if only a little bit. So I grabbed an orange slice on a toothpick, stepped into the street and started running backwards with the runners.

Zap! The force field came down; I could feel it. It was like night and day. Everyone started taking oranges from me. Suddenly, I became somebody who wasn't on the sidelines but expending some energy just like they were. Some of the athletes recognized me, the OxiClean guy, running with them and holding out something cold and full of sugar, and they couldn't turn it down. After they ate it, some said they didn't know what to do with the rind, and I said, "Don't worry, OxiClean will clean it up!" After I gave out one slice, I would run back, get another slice, run back out, and another runner would take it. Then I started running next to two runners holding two slices, one in each hand.

Just like that, the take-up went from 10 percent to 90 percent of runners that came by. The pitch was still the same; I was chanting, "Nice cold, ice cold oranges, Vitamin C, no pain, no gain, pain is temporary, pride is forever, have an orange, get you on your way, Vitamin C for the runners!" But running with them, empathizing with them—that was magic. As a sometime triathlete,I know what it feels like to be at that mark when everything hurts, and I knew how much a little burst of sugar would help. We went from giving away no oranges to all my oranges being gone in thirty minutes.

My mum thought this was super exciting, and next thing, I've got my mother running backwards with oranges shouting, "Nice, cold, ice cold!" Then my neighbors across the street, Steve and Rita, saw all this happening and loved the hoopla, so they went inside and started cutting up oranges and apples. Then the Shamrocks got into the act! They grabbed some fruit, butchered all my lines, and started running next to me. So now I had my mom, my stepfather, Mr. and Mrs. Shamrock, and my neighbors across the street all going, "Ice cold, nice cold, Vitamin C, California navel oranges!" See, that's good pitching: they're not just *oranges*, they're *ice-cold California navel oranges.* Alliteration and detail are your friends.

Before I knew what was happening, the whole neighborhood was into it, with my neighbors rolling out coolers packed with ice and fruit, running down the street after these triathletes, shouting and trying to hand them apple and melon slices. It was touching and funny and the enthusiasm was completely contagious.

THE REVEAL

This was an experiment in the difference between just standing there, letting people maintain their distance and protective force field, and pitching. There's an enormous difference between just standing around and being passive, which allows people's natural sales resistance and protective instinct to remain intact, and taking something to them on a physical and emotional level. You have to make a personal connection, to take things beyond the purely transactional. That's the Pitch Power I call . . .

BREACH THE FORCE FIELD

It may seem strange to look at it this way, but I was making a spiritual connection with these athletes. I was running with them and empathizing with them. I had closed the distance. When you just stand around trying to hand people things, it doesn't work because you're also in your own safe space. You're keeping yourself at a distance, so why shouldn't the other person do the same thing? To connect, you don't just breach the other person's force field; you have to breach your own, too.

That day, there was an emotional connection because I had left my safe cocoon and was feeling their pain just a tiny bit. There was a physical connection because I was running along with them. Then I had people saying, "Are you the OxiClean guy?" That was the kicker right there. They're like, *OMG, it's the OxiClean guy and he's running and giving me oranges!*

Another overlooked part of this is that reaching out like this is *fun*. Going out and connecting with these runners, seeing my mother doing it, seeing my neighbors getting into the act, seeing the surprise and gratitude on the runners' faces—it was fun. And when you're having fun, so will the person you're

THE PERSUADER!

Your product is really awesome. So awesome that it sells itself. It's the iPhone, Pokémon Go, and the new Harry Potter book rolled into one. For your next big trade show, you figure you can save money by sending a cheap staff of interns to man your booth because you won't need a pitchman to get people to place orders.

The Persuader says: "Bad idea. There's no such thing as a product that sells itself. A product can be amazing, but that doesn't mean people will stop in their tracks to check it out. The force field keeps them moving. You need charismatic people who know how to bally a tip to get people out of their bubble—basically, to stoke their curiosity so it overcomes their sales resistance—if you want to move units or hand out samples. Even the coolest product will never be more persuasive than a good pitchman."

pitching. Retail fails when people sit in a store and wait for the customers to come to them. That's why when I go to trade shows in Europe, I'll pass booths and you'll have these Israeli girls running up to you every five seconds with some pitch or bit of swag. They have to stand there for hours anyway, so why not work harder, have fun, engage the customer—and, by the way, get better results?

My triathlon experience took me right back to the crux of what the pitch is about, which is engagement on every level. I got super satisfied customers, and I knew it because the way the course runs, the competitors had to run back by my house heading for the finish line. They ran by, waving and shouting, "Hey!" Before, they were just four thousand men and women I didn't know. Now I had four thousand new friends.

Anatomy of a Superpower

This Pitch Power hinges on two basic truths:

Truth #1: It doesn't matter if what you're giving away is free if you're not enjoying yourself while you're giving it away. Think about Las Vegas. When you walk down the Strip, there are guys standing around giving out pamphlets, some of them actually *not* for the services of agile and enthusiastic young professional ladies. But nine times out of ten, people won't take the pamphlet. It's not heavy, and it doesn't cost anything, but we just don't want to deal with it because it's threatening our no-selling perimeter and activating the force field.

The big reason nobody takes the pamphlets is that those guys never smile or say anything. They just slap those damned pamphlets—*whack! whack! whack!*—and it sounds like gunshots. That doesn't work. If you want people to take that pamphlet, read it, and maybe use that 10 percent–off coupon from that restaurant, open your mouth. It doesn't matter if you don't speak English; chatter or sing in your native language. Open up. *Smile*. Show your pearly whites. Smiling is a natural human impulse; when we see a smile, we tend to smile back. Plus, research shows that smiling, even a fake smile, actually alters brain activity, reduces stress, and improves mood. So smile!

I love the guys who hold those four-foot arrow-shaped signs on street corners and busy roads. You've seen them. The signs are usually shaped like arrows and typically advertise a housing development or new business, and the best sign guys are amazing pitchmen. The sign guy isn't getting paid any more to dance, but he has to stand there for eight hours, so why not have some fun doing it? So he starts working that sign. You love the guy; you want to stop and give him a tip just because he's putting on a show on the sidewalk. He twirls it. He throws it in the air. He whips it behind his back like LeBron James on a breakaway. He's got his music, he's got his groove on, and he's getting a workout.

People look down at someone holding a sign on the corner of an intersection, but they actually *admire* the guy who's spinning it and laying down all the moves. Why? Because he's bringing it. He's in a shitty job and yet he's making the most of it. He's rising above his situation. We love that. He's like the cheerleader of sign work. He's pitching and *attracting* attention, not waiting for attention to come to him. The best pitchmen and pitchwomen are *attractive*.

That's pitching. That's reaching across the distance and breaking through somebody's protective bubble—and when somebody is a hundred feet away, in a metal and glass car going forty-five miles an hour, that's a hard bubble to break. If you've ever driven in California, you see the same thing. When you come down a freeway off-ramp and you're waiting at the stoplight at the bottom, you'll often see a street vendor on the concrete median selling flowers, oranges, or nuts. It's a way to make some extra cash. But ninety-nine out of a hundred of those guys just stand there and wait for somebody to open their car window. Most commuters won't do it because of the force field. The vendors I've seen who kill it, who sell every orange or bunch of carnations they have, are the ones who bring a guitar and sing Mexican folk songs. Or they stand there smiling and sing silly stuff about oranges. They might be tired, cold, and sick of breathing exhaust fumes, but they're having fun, and they're connecting. They're making it feel like you've got to have those oranges—so people buy them. It works *every single time*.

Truth #2: The best way to breach the force field is to make physical contact. The force field is about physical protection, about keeping our "personal space" clear of anyone we fear might try to take away our control to make our own choices. It's not impossible, but it is very difficult to get through someone's personal bubble without engaging with them physically in some way.

With the triathletes outside my house, I knew how to do that because I've been where they were. I know how much it sucks to do a 1500-meter swim, a 40-kilometer bike ride, and a 10-kilometer run. It's hot, and if you're an amateur, you've been going for who knows how long. In the first half of the run, you're running away from the finish line, and that's the darkest point of the race. You also don't want water because people are handing out water all over the course. You don't want Gatorade. Oranges are cold and chewy and full of natural sugar, and I knew the runners would love them.

Running with them made all the difference because I did 99 percent of the work to close that physical gap, and at the same time I was closing the spiritual gap by suffering along with them just a little bit. Once they decided to reach for that orange, even though there was a fork or a cocktail stick stuck in it, the physical connection clicked. We connected on a physical level, similar to the way I connect with people live when I hand out product. You get them to hold the product and they start nodding. It becomes real.

WITH GREAT POWER COMES GREAT RESPONSIBILITY

This Pitch Power makes some people uncomfortable. But that's good. We've become complacent about getting out into the world and reaching out to people, because we think

INCOMPETENT SIDEKICK: THE OVERSELLER

This loser gets you in trouble by overdoing the pitch so that the person on the other end feels pressured and uncomfortable. You see Oversellers at timeshare sales events and anyplace where men and women are looking at jewelry. They never seem to understand that making eye contact does not necessarily mean you want to buy. Don't let this sidekick trip you up. Nobody wants to be harangued or pressured.

we can do it from the safety of a laptop keyboard or smartphone screen. But that's not true. Facebook friends aren't real friends. Communicating with someone by way of posts and tweets and emoji is nothing like seeing their body language, making them smile, or sharing a laugh with an entire crowd. A kind of collective hug becomes possible when people are in the same space together that isn't possible when we're at a distance.

Are we safer from people who might disagree with us? Sure. Is it more convenient to roll out of bed and "like" something on Facebook than to get dressed, go out in the cold morning air, and say to people, "Sir, how do you mop your floors?" Of course. But we're poorer for it. If you distance yourself or kid yourself that you can connect with people from a piece of backlit glass, you'll never learn to pitch and never reap all the benefits.

But still . . . scary. We like our physical space. So it's a good thing that actually touching someone physically is not the only way to breach their force field. Now to be fair, it's still the *best* way. Physical contact or a physical exchange—taking an orange slice, handling a product, passing a sample around an audience—are still your most effective tools for creating that immediate sense of intimacy. I'm not talking about feeling people up, but the act of subtle touch. If you have an opportunity to engage someone in a physical manner, engage them. I do it all the time: "Feel that, smell that, taste this. You want a free taste? Have a taste. We've got free samples today." You're giving someone a little cup and now you've involved a sense that wasn't previously involved.

But engaging someone physically is not appropriate in every situation, and not every audience is receptive to it. So you're in luck, because there are five—count 'em, five—other ways to break that barrier.

1. Make them laugh. On the triathlon course, I wasn't just screaming at the top of my voice about ice-cold oranges. I also offered the runners a free hose-down as they went by, and if you've ever run a 10k on a warm day, you know how good that cool water feels. But more than that, I was having a dig at some people all in fun. For instance, every athlete has a number, so you pick someone's number, or something that makes them stand out. and you cheer them on or make a mild joke. I remember one lady with a pink hat, wearing number 118. When she ran by I started chanting, "Pink Hat, go, Pink Hat, 1-1-8!" She knew she was wearing a pink hat, she was hurting, and she was happy that someone was cheering her on. It made everyone smile. I did the same when Alicia Kaye ran by, because even though she's a pro, I knew she was hurting, too. By the way, she took second among the women that day, which was awesome.

Everybody loves to smile. Make a big hoopla about what you've got. Find something about the person you're pitching to and poke a little light fun at them or what they're doing. For instance, say you're interviewing for a highly competitive job and you know the interviewer sitting across from you has already seen about a hundred candidates and is sick of the whole thing. You sit down, and before she can utter a word, you say with a wink and a grin, "I know you're sick of this, so I accept. I'll take the job. See? I just made your day easier." Nine times out of ten, I'll bet you get a smile or a laugh. Instant connection. The tenth? Well, you probably don't want to work for such a humorless sod anyway.

And never forget the value of self-deprecation. The best way to get that smile on someone's face and keep the laugh going is to make fun of yourself. That's what stand-up comedians do. That's why a lot of super intense salespeople get it wrong. So you go to a car lot. You get the guy we all dread: the always-on guy who knows everything about the car and expects you to be as excited about it as he is. You probably don't like him because he makes you feel pressured. But the guy who's funny, who makes you enjoy the process, who doesn't take the whole thing too seriously? Nine times out of ten he doesn't know precisely how many foot-pounds of torque the car puts out, but he's probably the one you're going to buy from.

2. Care. Show genuine concern about what you're doing and who you're doing it for. Don't just say you care; show it. This even works on television. On TV, you have no idea who's watching and no way to interact with them directly, so you have to make a strong impression that breaks the force field. For example, when I go on HSN, I make a concerted effort to tease the hosts in a way that shows I know and care about them. For instance, Robin Wall has been working there for twenty years, and she's one of a handful of people there who have climbed the ladder from hand model to show host. So every time I go on I compliment her about it, even though it makes her uncomfortable. When I come on, before we even get started, but live on camera, I always stop the pitch and tell Robin, "Robin, I'm so proud of you. Look at you."

She'll say, "Stop it," but I'll ignore her, turn to the customers at home, and say, "Did you know that Robin was a model and I've known her for twenty years?" Meanwhile, Robin is blushing and fidgeting behind me. Then I turn to her and gush, "Robin, I'm your biggest fan." It's banter, it's a ritual, it's innocent flirtation—and it works. It breaks the ice, and it works because people can see that I genuinely like Robin. If I didn't like her, everyone would know it. People aren't stupid. But it's real, and we're having fun, so the viewer is having fun.

3. Recruit co-conspirators. You know the saying "There are no atheists in foxholes?" There are also no atheists in audiences when the speaker says the words "audience participation." Everyone starts praying, "*Don't pick me, don't pick me*" But when you pick someone to help you, they become a proxy for the entire audience. If you're pitching to a group, delivering a speech, or giving a performance, this is a great force field breaker. I used to do it when I pitched vegetable slicers in street markets. I would find a sweet-looking woman and just work on her: "Does anyone like onions? Do you like onions? Are these onions good? Open your bag, love, and let's see if you've got any onions." By now, she's giggling and everybody else is laughing with her. It's magic.

Once, I saw a guy selling a juicer in a street market and had a big tip watching him. At some point in my own pitches, I would always pass things into the crowd for people to hold and examine, and on this occasion this guy did the same thing, passing around fruit that could be juiced—oranges, lemons, limes—and asking people to squeeze the juice out of them.

Then he threw the crowd a curveball. He found this sweet little old woman, passed her an apple, and asked her to squeeze the juice out of it. Well, of course you can't squeeze juice from an apple, but the entire audience was howling as this lady squeezed and squeezed and nothing happened. Nobody was making fun; everybody was in on the joke. But by making her a part of his pitch, he'd made the entire audience part of it. By recruiting one person, he connected with fifty.

Try it. If you want to meet someone attractive in a bar, get her to help you prank your buddy. If you're pitching a potential client, instead of slides, bring oversized cards and ask someone from the client to hold them while you speak. If you're working on a customer service rep at the airport to get a first-class upgrade, promise to write a fantastic complimentary email about her to her superior if she hooks you up, and then do it. When you can make your audience your ally, you've got it made.

4. Be direct. Guess what? The girl you're hitting on knows you're hitting on her. Your supervisor knows you're in the office to try to get a raise. Don't be coy. When people think that *you* think they're too dumb to get that you're pitching them, they get angry. So be direct. You're trying to get the girl's phone number or you want a raise and a promotion. Your cards are on the table and you can play.

5. Have a secret. People love to be in on a secret. It gets them leaning forward in their chairs and transforms you into someone special. When I'm pitching, I always have a secret. It's the perfect way to change gears and vary your patter. "Why am I so good? Because I have a British accent. That's my secret. The reason I'm so good is because I have these blue eyes. They can melt people when I look at them. *That's* the secret. My real secret to success is getting up at 4:00 a.m. and working out. I'm in the office at 6:00 a.m. every single day. Before you even think about waking up, I'm already here working for you. That's the secret to my success." You can create a secret for any situation.

Try each of these methods to use this Pitch Power and bring down those barriers. When you're talking to that attractive woman at the club, invite her to join you in trying a special drink the bartender invented. If you're making your pitch to a group of customers, instead of letting them sit on their butts and watch another PowerPoint deck, make funny photo books about your company and pass one to each of them. If you're giving a speech and the room is dead, leave the podium and go sit with the audience, then keep talking. They'll love it.

Other times this Pitch Power can help you win the day and get the girl (or guy):

- **Getting better medical care.** Doctors and nurses distance themselves from patients because it helps them be more objective, but it can also result in cold, impersonal, crappy care, especially if you're hospitalized. Remember that they're human, probably very busy, and almost always stressed out. Be kind and find a way to connect—kids, school, a tattoo, something. They'll probably listen more closely and you might even get a private room, always a luxury.
- **Getting a hotel upgrade.** The same principle works here as with docs and nurses: when someone is constantly busy

and most people are berating them, stand out by being the person who reaches out and treats them like a human being. Breach the barrier that clerks put up to protect themselves from irate guests and engage—a simple compliment can do it. The more the person across the check-in desk likes you, the better your odds of getting that suite.

- **Talking your way out of a ticket.** I've done this, and it's not easy. Plus, the Pitch Powers don't work every time. But it's worth a shot. Cops keep themselves behind a protective wall, but if you're honest about why you were speeding or ran the light and even make the officer laugh, you stand a decent chance of getting off with a warning. At the very least, you won't exacerbate the bad news of a citation by being an asshole, too. Being a cop is tough. This cop is standing out in the cold or heat, worrying about getting shot. Cops get a ton of abuse, so do the opposite of what your gut is telling you to do. Own it, say you're sorry, admit it, and be cool. You have nothing to lose.

Story-Furthering Interlude

My friend Juls Bindi learned all about this Pitch Power. She invented a dog carrier called ZuGoPet. It's the Mercedes-Benz of dog carrying cases. She sold them on Amazon but she wasn't moving much product. On a trip to LA, I stayed in her spare bedroom and it was stacked to the ceiling with ZuGoPets in boxes. I told her she had to get rid of the inventory and she said, "I know, I know, I'm getting rid of it slowly." I knew this was a job for Pitchman. The next morning, I gave her a master class in pitching.

Juls is passionate about her product, and it solves lots of problems. But it's $199. If you just put a pet carrier on a table at that price, people are going to walk by, look at the price tag, and keep walking. I told her, "Right. First things first: you need to bally your tip, or gather a group of buyers around you. The best way to do that is to have a dog with you. People will just come over to pet the dog. Bring Russell (that's her dog). Russell is going to be 'Russell the Muscle.' He's going to bally your tip for you."

She looked at me like I was nuts. "Really?"

"Absolutely," I said. "You're going to have one dog carrier out and all the colors—pink, black, white—stacked up behind you. Get a light on them so everything else around you looks dark. Get something to stand on so you're elevated. And don't wait for people to come to you. Start talking to them: 'Do you have a dog, I have a dog, come on over. Do you want to pet the dog, do you want to pet the dog?' Don't waste your time pitching to people who don't have dogs or don't know someone who has a dog."

Then I told her to tell a story. Did you know the number-two cause of automobile accidents is dogs being in the back of the car unrestrained, distracting their drivers? Neither did I, and neither do dog owners. Then I told her to get into how the bag solved problems. When the dog walks inside, it has a blanket. The bag has mesh panels so the dog can see out. You can hang it between the two seats so if you get rear-ended the dog won't go flying into the windshield. I said, "Get familiar with your product to the point where you can pick it up and maneuver it blindfolded."

Next, get *fierce agreement*. While you're talking, you're getting people to agree with what you say about your product. Ask people the name of their dog—let's say it's Buster—and you say, "Doesn't this look like Buster would be comfortable in this?" Yes, they'll say. "Looks like he'd be pretty safe in it, too." They'll nod.

Finally, I told Juls to hand the bags to every person in the crowd and give them a reason to want to hold them. "Hand them out and say, 'Which color do you want? Feel the quality of this. Feel how light this is.'" People will get the bag and heft it and marvel to each other, "Oh, feel how light this is." I always laugh at people's suggestibility. Of course it's light—it's a little leather satchel! Now you're handing people the dog carrier they just heard all about in the color they want. Finally, the ask, "Would anybody like to know the price?" You're not telling them the price. You're *asking* them if they'd *like* to know the price. They will *always* say yes.

I went on for forty-five minutes, and she and her assistant were feverishly taking notes. Then I flew home, and the next thing I knew I got a call from Juls, shouting, "You made me a millionaire!" Apparently, she took the bags to a show in Las Vegas and used everything I taught her. I'll let her finish the story:

"I started ZuGoPet in 2010 with the sole purpose of helping our rescue dogs with anxiety and keeping them safe while they travel," Juls says. "With a lack of innovative products on the market, I decided to make my own. Then came Sully. I met him in Mexico through a mutual friend, Thom Beers. We hit it off and he loved my product, and when Sully loves a product he's gung ho and wants to jump in and help.

"When he stayed with me in LA, he let me record the pitch so I could listen to it over and over again and get it right," she continues. "When I was preparing for SuperZoo, the world's largest pet show, I swore I was not going to let Sully or myself down. I was going to sell the doggie doo-doo out of these products. I wasn't nervous at all! I saw Sully standing right there saying, 'Time to get their hands raised!'

'Pass out the product . . . 3 . . . 2 . . . 1 . . . *now!*'

'Tell them what they love about the bag!'

'Ask them their pet's name!'

'Ask them to pitch it to the person standing next to them!'

'Ask them how much they would pay for it!'

"My boyfriend, my designer, and her husband stood back, wide-eyed, watching me take over and sell out," she concludes. "Following Sully's steps, it came as second nature. I was officially a pitchwoman, and good at it! Sully's approach is so obvious once he explains it: put on a show and make them want to pay for it at the end. Not only are they getting an amazing product but they just watched a flawless performance that they will come back to see again."

Plot Twist!

Juls did amazing, especially for her first time using this Pitch Power, which is hard. You have your own force field and it can be frightening to breach it. But it's even worse when you use some of these tricks to close that distance and take down that barrier, and the other person stares at you like you're a bug on a pin.

Like all the Pitch Powers, this one is only one tool in your arsenal. It's a powerful one, but you need to be careful to use it when it's appropriate. In some situations, and with some people, you want to keep your distance and keep them at theirs. For instance, there have been times when I've been talking to lawyers, in my personal life and professional life, that I did *not* want them warming up to me. I knew all the pitching in the world wasn't going to make a difference, and I didn't want them to get the misconception that I was trying to manipulate them. Likewise, I've been in negotiations where I had to play my cards close to the vest. If you have too much fun, you can relax and say something you shouldn't. Let the other guy make the mistakes, not you.

Most of the time, making physical contact, humor, or having a secret will work wonders to break that protective bubble and warm people up. But use these tricks to know when you should leave them cold:

- **Watch body language.** This is the big one. Breaking eye contact, restless hands, forced laughter, people looking at each other—these are all cues that your routine is falling flat. Back off FAST and be serious and direct.
- **Note the environment.** Is the room set up so that you're deliberately at a physical distance from the other person? Are you one of many applicants? Is the bar so loud that any funny lines are barely audible? Maybe not the place for barrier breaking.
- **Throw out some bait.** Finally, try throwing out some test lines to see what happens. If you learn that the other person's birthday is a few days away, say something like "I noticed your birthday is on Saturday. Got any big plans?" If they look surprised and delighted, you're golden. If they react like you're a stalker, apologize for being intrusive and hope they forget it happened.

Training Montage

It doesn't matter if you're selling cars or making sales calls on a buyer. It doesn't matter if you're hitting on someone hot or trying to film a Kickstarter video that will get people to give you $25,000 for your invention. *You will hit a wall of sales resistance.* If you're coming into my office to sit across a desk from me and try to sell me shit that I don't want, you should

WHAT WOULD BILLY DO?

Billy Mays here! What would I do if I dropped one of my classic lines (I would ask people where they were from and then say, "My mother was from Iceland, my father was from Cuba. I'm an ice cube") on someone and they just stared back, stone faced? First, I'd stop. Then I'd make fun of myself for being clumsy enough to drop a joke into a meeting where it clearly wasn't appropriate. Then I'd shut up. But I'd be observing the other guy. I like to have fun and work with people with a sense of humor. Do I want this guy as my boss or my customer? Maybe not. Smart pitching also means knowing when you're pitching the wrong person.

expect that. However, novice pitching superheroes are always shocked when people don't even want things they're giving away for free.

That's the force field, and the best way to learn to breach it is to practice giving something away for free in public. I'm serious. On a hot day, get a cooler full of frozen orange slices, go out to a busy recreational trail where hundreds of people are walking, running, and cycling, and try to give them away. Anyone who is afraid or thinks they can't pitch can do exactly what I did. At first, people won't take what you're offering. Try what I've taught you in this chapter. By the end of the day, you'll have figured out how to break the ice with people. If you practice anything long enough, you'll get good at it.

You'll also conquer that perfectly normal moment of fear, that stage fright that comes when you step out of *your* force field. Go to a road race, find a quiet corner, and cut up a bunch of oranges. Everyone's going to be super grateful. So you get a rejection? A runner runs by you. You're never going to see them again. But you're going to have so many take-ups and smiles and so much interaction. It's a genuine human transaction. You're solving a problem for these people for what? The cost of an orange. If you can't sell it, practice giving it away for free. Once you've perfected giving it away for free and you're really good at it, then maybe you can graduate to actually asking for money. That's how you learn to pitch.

SCENARIOS FOR USING THE "BREACH THE FORCE FIELD" PITCH POWER

Q: *You tell someone a joke and they look offended. What do you do?*

A: Fall on your sword. You've just touched a negative emotion, which is powerful stuff. So you reframe the joke and say, "I'm sorry. I'm just rather nervous right now and I thought I could defuse it by telling a joke. Obviously, that wasn't a good idea. Can we start over again?"

Q: *You see someone attractive in a public place but he or she has a wingman (or woman). Do you move on, ignore the friend, or turn him/her into your ally?*

A: Ally, always. Now, if you're with a friend and you can get him or her to charm the wingman, that's ideal. But if you're not, turn the wing-person into your advocate. Be charming and warm and genuine to both of them, so that when you excuse yourself to go to the bathroom, the friend turns to the object of your affections and says, "He's a catch! Go for it!" instead of "Quick, let's leave before he gets back!"

Q: *You're giving out orange slices (or something) when the police tell you to stop. Do you leave with your tail between your legs or pretend to leave and set up shop elsewhere?*

A: A pitchman never quits. Find a new place to pitch—and work the police episode into your new pitch! "The cops tried to stop me because what I'm giving away is so great it should be illegal." That sort of thing.

POWER NUMBER SIX

FACTS TELL, STORIES SELL

Good for saving the day in public speaking, making your case for a raise or promotion, closing a new customer, or killing it in a sales presentation.

WHEN WE LAST LEFT OUR HERO . . .

You were trying to figure out which makes you more uncomfortable: sticking your neck out to break a stranger's force field or bombing at your attempt to sell, convince, or meet them. While you figure that out, let me tell you a story about storytelling.

ORIGIN STORY

One of the best pitches I ever gave involved telling a story to someone I wasn't even supposed to be talking to. It also didn't involve pitching but *storytelling*. It was 2007, I was going through a divorce, and I was in a crappy place mentally and emotionally. One of the only silver linings on my horizon was that Billy Mays and I were about to get a deal on a reality show. We had shot a "sizzle reel" and run it up the chain at Warner Brothers, and they loved it. We got a call from the then head of New Programming Development, Brooke Karzen, who said, "We love you, we love Billy, we love the whole concept for the show. We'll give you $20,000 an episode and we want to sign you as soon as possible." This was the show that became *Pitchmen.*

At the time, I was planning a weeklong getaway at a wellness retreat called the Ashram in Calabasas, California—some time to get my head together. I kicked the contract over to my attorney, who ran down Brooke and told me she was the real deal. The plan was that when I got back to LA, we would sign the deal. I called Billy and told him the good news, and everything was hunky-dory.

I went to the Ashram. It's a spartan wellness retreat. There were only thirteen other people staying there, and one of the cardinal rules of the place is *no business*. No networking, no deal making, no handing out business cards. But on day one, at the end of the dining table was a guy I didn't know. He was a character, talking a million miles an hour about *Monster Garage* and *Deadliest Catch.* He was obviously in the cable TV business, but I was not there to do business and neither was he. He was just talking about his life.

But the next day, I couldn't stop trying to figure out who he was. On the doors of your room, the Ashram only puts your first name and the first initial of your last name and his door read THOM B. *I have to find out who this guy is.* I used my cell phone (against the rules) and called my assistant in Florida. I said, "Google *'Monster Garage, Thom B.'* Find out who this guy is." It turned out that he was Thom Beers, executive producer of *Deadliest Catch* and *Ice Road Truckers,* at the time the biggest swinging dick in the cable reality show business.

Now, I've got this show that I am about to sell to Warner Brothers. But now I'm thinking that it might be worth having a conversation with Beers about our show. At the same time, I realize that he's at a wellness yoga retreat, so the last thing he probably wants to hear is a pitch for a TV show. So, I had two challenges for my pitching prowess:

A: Find my moment.

B: When I find my moment, don't fuck it up.

I decided that before I tried to pitch Beers, I would get to know him (but I wouldn't tell him who I was). He wasn't the fittest guy at the Ashram, but I'm fairly fit, so when we did our daily hikes, I was always at the front of the pack. But starting on the third day, I began hanging back with Thom. We did this really steep hill called Bulldog, and I ended up climbing it with him and talking, and I got inside his head. I found out who he was, what he did, and it turned out that the best man at his wedding was my old boss. It was all very serendipitous.

Still, three more days went by and I never brought up the reality show. I was cutting it down to the wire. On the sixth day, I knew I had to make my move. We were both relaxing in the swimming pool and we'd become kind of friendly and—remember the scene in *Apocalypse Now* where Martin Sheen rises out of the water in his camouflage face paint on the way to kill Marlon Brando? Think about that, minus the machete and camo.

I went underwater and I had a little conversation with myself, gave myself a pep talk. Then I came out of the water at about the same speed as Martin Sheen in that scene, swam over to Thom, took a deep breath, and said, "Thom, I know you probably don't want to hear this, but I feel like I have to tell you this story." His face took on a weary "here we go" expression, but I pushed on. Sometimes, you just have to be confident and go for it.

I asked if he knew Billy Mays. He said yes. I told him Billy was my partner and we'd put together a sizzle reel for a reality show and that Warner Brothers had offered to pay us $20,000 an episode. "The minute I leave the Ashram," I said, "the first thing I'm going to do is call my attorney and we're going to sign a deal for this show. I just figured, based on everything that you do, I had to talk to you to see if we're making the right move." The whole thing took thirty seconds.

He looked at me, and if there was ever a moment when he could have walked away and gotten me busted for talking business, that was it. But he didn't. He said, "What's the premise of the show?" I gave him a half minute of backstory while he was getting out of the pool. By the time I was done, he had already turned his back on me and I could tell he didn't want to hear any more about it. I made my case in about half a minute because I knew that's all I would get. Thom then walked into the Ashram without another word, leaving me with only the hope that I'd made a good impression.

Critical Components

I didn't dare pitch Thom or he would've gotten pissed, shut down, and walked away immediately. I had to tell him a story, and every single world out of my mouth was critical and strategic:

"Billy Mays and I are going to have this show; we don't know the title yet."

"Warner Brothers."

"Twenty thousand dollars an episode."

"The minute I leave the Ashram, I'm going to go back and sign a deal."

I knew exactly what I was going to say and I cut it off at thirty seconds. I knew I had to hook him with the vital details and let him know I was a player, not some wannabe with a script in my room. Every piece of my story had a purpose; I wasn't just sharing information. But after he left I sat by the pool, thinking, *Well, Sully, you fucked that up. He's pissed off at you.*

An hour later, he came back and sat down near me. He didn't say anything for a second, and then went, "Billy Mays, tell me more about him." *Yes. I've got a hook!* I started talking about Billy and me and our work together. After a few minutes, I went for it: I asked if he wanted to see the sizzle reel. First, he said no. As I said, the Ashram absolutely forbids doing business—no phones, no computers, and definitely no sizzle reels. Also, there are copyright issues; if he saw our reel, we could accuse him of stealing it if he came up with a similar show on his own. Then he said, "Let's show the sizzle reel to the whole Ashram." I ran to get my computer and we played it for everyone there.

Everybody loved it, and Thom was in. The next day, we got out of relaxation mode and went into how we were going to take over the world with this new show. We sat on the floor of the Ashram with a piece of paper, instructing each other about our worlds: him teaching me about reality TV and me teaching him about pitching, inventions, and direct sales. Business, business, business.

The owner of the Ashram, a Swedish woman named Katarina, was furious with us for flouting the "no business" rule over and over. She threatened to kick us out, and then when that didn't work made us promise that if the show got picked up, we would buy her a car. No problem. We got the show, and eventually we bought Katarina a Mercedes-Benz, as promised.

THE REVEAL

Thom Beers did not want to be sold. He was at the Ashram to chill out and take a break from business. So I didn't pitch him. First, I got to know him a little. Then when I made my move, I grabbed him with the story of me, Billy, and our idea. I wove a little sixty-second drama complete with two main characters, a conflict, and something at stake. I didn't ask him for anything; I just told a story, which is one of the most naturally human activities there is. In fact, it qualifies as a Pitch Power that I call . . .

FACTS TELL, STORIES SELL

Don't get me wrong; facts are important. But people aren't as rational as we like to think we are. Research shows that much of the time when we make a decision to buy something like a car, we choose what satisfies our emotions—a $125,000 Tesla roadster, for example—and then use facts to rationalize the choice after the fact. So buying the Tesla becomes all about zero emissions and climate change and has *nothing* to do with driving a butt rocket that goes zero to sixty in four seconds flat.

Facts, data, and evidence might give someone a reason to say yes, but what gets him to listen to your pitch in the first place and to like you enough to want to do business with you is the

THE PERSUADER!

The benefits of your product are blindingly obvious. Your merits as a job candidate are right there on your resume. Why go to the trouble of telling a story? Why not just inform your listener about how awesome your product is or how experienced and trustworthy you are?

The Persuader says: "You could do that, but it's a novice move. True pitching superheroes know they're not pitching in a vacuum. The person or group you're addressing might have already heard the same salesmanship from twenty other people before you. There's not much new that you can say—except your story. Your story is unique, because nobody's lived your life. That uniqueness is a superpower. Plus, when you talk about what you did or who you helped, it's like having a narrator describing your achievements instead of you. It's more objective. Plus, your listeners can fact-check your story if they choose. All that adds up to make you more credible and interesting."

stuff that appeals to his curiosity, empathy, sense of humor, and love of a happy ending: *storytelling*. Facts might convince someone to take a chance on you, but appealing to emotions by telling a great story brings down sales resistance and gets you in the door in the first place.

The trick is, it's not enough just to drop a story on someone. As you saw with Thom Beers, it has to be the right story at the right time, told the right way. An irrelevant or meandering story might have your listener rolling her eyes and checking her watch, sure signs that you've lost your audience. Let's look at what makes a good story, and how to tell it.

Anatomy of a Superpower

Storytelling is an important part of being human. For most of our history, wisdom was passed on by oral tradition: grandmother to granddaughter, village elder sitting around at a town hall meeting. It wasn't until we invented writing that we gained the ability to pass on stories to anyone but the one or two generations that were right in front of us. But storytelling is a bit of a lost art today. Everybody's staring at their phones all the time, texting, and there's that horrible shorthand "tl;dr," which means "too long; didn't read." Nobody takes the time to interact anymore, which is ironic because there's such a deep pleasure in sitting down around a campfire and listening to someone tell a great story. It's a mythical talent. Campfire storytelling. In sales, "Let me tell you a story" normally comes after everyone's had a couple of drinks, but it's the same, very human, need.

I've been told I'm a great storyteller, and I do think a good story will bail you out of any situation. But it's not a cure-all. Storytelling is an art form. You've got to keep your story on point, close to the sale, and don't let it turn into a yarn. For me to want to listen to your story, at least one of the following has to be working for you:

1. **Relevance.** Your story should mean something to me and contain something that relates to my life, my challenges, or something I want. Thom Beers stopped to listen to my pool pitch because in telling him about the TV show Billy and I were on the verge of selling, I was talking about his world. It was relevant to him, and it didn't hurt that in coming to him with the story, I was also subtly asking for his advice, which is respectful and flattering.

Here's what I mean. When I pitch my steam cleaner on HSN, I always stop my presentation and say, "Let me tell you a story." I start talking about when I was eighteen years old, working for $4 an hour at the Vacation Inn on the North Shore of Oahu for this lady named Sharlyn (hi, Shar!). I got paid to clean up after fifty surfers, so I know what it's like to clean in a pigsty. I say, "If you think you know what it's like to clean a toilet after boys have used it, imagine cleaning up after fifty surfers who only care about smoking weed, drinking beer, and meeting girls." I tell viewers that the bleach made all my body hair turn white, but that I got the job done and it was the happiest I've ever been in my whole life.

I close by mentioning that I went to see Sharlyn in February of 2016 when I dislocated my shoulder, and she gave me a ration of shit about it. Viewers are thinking, *Wow, Sully worked there for four bucks an hour thirty years ago and he keeps up a relationship with this woman?* It's a quick anecdote that's true, gets people laughing, and builds respect because people know that I've cleaned toilets, just like them. That's such a great story that when I'm on HSN and there's a lull, the producer will say, "Tell the Hawaii story," because it works.

2. Humor, especially at your expense. Remember, we all love to laugh. We all love to be entertained, and being funny sometimes matters more than being skilled. If you've traveled in any big city, then you've probably seen street performers, or "buskers" as they call them in Europe. Great buskers are amazing pitchmen, because while they're delivering funny lines and commanding the attention of a crowd with charisma and confidence, they're juggling flaming chainsaws or some such thing! But I see the same pattern with buskers, be they acrobats, musicians, magicians, or what have you: the funny ones get bigger crowds and bigger tips than the technically skilled ones who don't tell jokes—or worse, go through their routine with a stone-faced expression. We like to laugh, feel like part of a special group, and be entertained.

It's even better if the humor makes you the butt of the joke. I do this on HSN all the time. Say I'm pitching my steam cleaner. I could tell viewers all about it being a great mop that'll absorb everything, but it works much better when I tell them about the time (this is true) that my toilet exploded at 4:00 a.m. and I used the mop to clean up all the water that kept welling up out of it. They can picture me in my pajamas, ankle deep in water, and they love it.

3. Universal drama. In August of 2016, I crashed my racing bike going about thirty miles an hour. I went down hard on my left side, and the only reason I didn't end up with a vicious compound fracture of my arm was that for some reason, I maintained the presence of mind to keep my arm tucked in and take the impact on my shoulder, fracturing my scapula. But as fun as that was, it was an eye opener to go to the ER and see that my Giro bike helmet had completely split open from the impact. In other words, it had done what it was supposed to do: absorb the energy so my head wouldn't. If I hadn't been wearing it, I probably would not have written this book.

Because of that experience I could go on air tomorrow and sell bike helmets, because I can tell a real-world story that's full of drama. Even if they've never wiped out on a bike, they've had some sort of close call or know somebody who has. They can relate and they have empathy for me. I don't know when I'll use that story in a pitch, but I know I will.

4. Likability. Even if a story doesn't have a ton to do with me, isn't dramatic, and isn't very funny, I'll listen for a long time if I like you. That's one of the reasons my Hawaii story about cleaning up after surfers resonates. Viewers who only know me as Sully the pitchman who does OxiClean commercials find out that I've done crap jobs, lived in a van, and know how to poke fun at myself. They like me. It's really that simple. I don't put on airs or distance myself from them; I intentionally paint word pictures where I make myself look ridiculous. I tease my co-hosts and let them tease me. I make it very clear that other than a preternatural ability to talk about mops and vegetable slicers with unnerving enthusiasm, I'm exactly like them. That makes them willing to put up with some storytelling, and you'll find the same to be true for you.

However, the ability to be an effective storyteller—hold up, what does that mean? Is there a difference between telling a *good* story and an *effective* one? You bet there is. A good story is entertaining and captivating, but that's all it is, and there's nothing wrong with that. But you're here to learn to be a pitching superhero, and that means *persuasion with a purpose*. Telling an effective story means there's a purpose behind it: breaking the ice, prepping someone to hear your pitch, driving home your experience or knowledge—something. Effective storytelling happens with an outcome in mind.

Where was I? Right, effective storytelling. At the end of the day, it's about *trust*. Think about it: why do you spend money on books by your favorite authors? In part, it's because you trust that the storytelling of John Grisham, Bill Bryson, or whoever won't waste your money or your time. It is the same when you're telling a story in person, except that you have maybe thirty seconds to gain your listener's trust. When your

INCOMPETENT SIDEKICK: BLUE BABBLER

In the stand-up comedy world, "blue" means profane. Foul language might be fine for a Las Vegas stage (and I love using it in private), but it's rarely a good idea when you're pitching. By dropping f-bombs into your stories, this sidekick makes you seem vulgar and inarticulate, and shocks listeners right out of any spell you were weaving. Sure, every now and then it's perfectly fine to drop in a swear work, depending on your audience. It can even make a point stronger. But use blue language in your stories like you use booze in your cooking: sparingly.

story is detailed, well paced, self-deprecating, concise, and relevant to them, you make deposits to your trust bank account. The more you make, the longer they'll listen.

WITH GREAT POWER COMES GREAT RESPONSIBILITY

The thing is, earning that trust doesn't happen by accident. Storytellers—especially when the story is a part of an effective pitch—are made, not born. There's a specific set of tools you need to work with if you're going to make the transition from someone who might be good at telling funny stories at a party to a pitching superhero who can use stories strategically to persuade people to give you what you want. The first tool is understanding the *beats* of a story.

You hear the word "beat" used all the time about stage acting and public speaking, but what are they? Beats are those tiny pauses when what's being said changes from one thing to another. They're transitions that you can feel. But it's not enough to know when a transition is coming; you need to know what comes next. Here's a quick primer on the beats of a great pitching story:

1. **The vivid setup.** You have to grab the listener's attention immediately or you'll lose them. Talk about what's at stake in the story, the obstacles, tickle their funny bone, or something. But you have to rivet them right away. After you have them at your mercy, transition to the next beat.
2. **Characters.** They have to know who the players are in your story. Who's who? What is each person like and why do they do what they do? The story won't be as meaningful or have as much impact if your audience doesn't understand the nature, background, or flaws in the people you're talking about, even if that's just you.
3. **Turning point.** At some point, your story has to shift to a moment of truth when the main character either reaches his or her goal, fails to reach it, or experiences something surprising. For me with Thom Beers in the pool, the turning point came when I told him that Billy and I had a TV deal . . . but we weren't sure we would accept it.
4. **Takeaway.** The last beat is when you get to what you want the listener to take away from your story, usually some kind of lesson. The idea here is either to teach the reader something about you or teach them a truth or idea that will make them more receptive to the rest of your pitch.

Learning where these beats fall, how to recognize them, and how to smoothly switch from one to the next takes practice and time, which is why I encourage you not only to work on your own storytelling but to listen to great storytellers whenever you can: salesmen, speakers, even preachers. Hear the cadences and rhythms and note when the speaker switches from one beat to the next—it's obvious when you're looking for it, like a train changing tracks.

Framing

Framing is about making those beats more effective. Effective pitching isn't throwing meaningless detail at the listener; that just confuses and irritates them. Instead, you use context and detail to lend reality and depth to the story and to help people see and feel the value in what you're offering. The more you speak in terms that engage the listener's other senses—in words they can see, smell, feel, and bite into—the more you keep them engaged in your story. When you do it right, you can completely reframe what your audience hears and how they feel.

That's what I did with my friend Reno Rollé and his green superfood product, Boku. A few years ago, he came to my company with this product, a blend of superfoods that you're supposed to blend and drink. Well, there are a million similar products out there, but my job was to make his unique. He had cue cards and more product than you could shake a stick at, and he wanted me to come up with this magical pitch that we could build an infomercial around. Stumped, I said, "Put all your shit on the table and let's work the problem."

Days went by and I kept striking out. I was looking for the "hook," but I couldn't find it. Meanwhile, Reno was talking about how the Latin root of the word "protein" is *protean*, which means healthy and vital. Who gives a shit? We needed to hit people where they live. We needed to bypass their logical brain, where sales resistance lives, and get to their reptilian brain, where emotions like fear and disgust set up shop. Engage their emotions.

One night, we were at dinner, sitting around over a bottle of wine and talking about sketches. We got to talking about the famous Bass-O-Matic sketch from *Saturday Night Live*, in which Dan Ackroyd does a hilarious parody of a TV pitchman selling a blender, pulverizes a real fish in the thing, and then drinks it! It was a disgusting, pants-wetting funny but, and it hit me. I said, "I've got it. We're going to run with this. We're going to try it. We're going to get a blender, put everything in it that most people eat for a day, and turn it on. Then we're going to pour it out and say, 'You want to know why you feel awful? This is why.'"

The table lit up like a Christmas tree. Everybody started laughing and suggesting things that we could put in the blender: beer, a doughnut, a Pop-Tart, a piece of pizza, a soda, and a hot dog. Any of the typical high-fat, high-sugar, fast-food garbage that the typical American eats. We'd put in there and blend it all into the nastiest sludge imaginable. Boku would be the alternative to the "get fat, feel terrible, die young" diet!

Now we had a great product and a terrific ice breaker. We wrote the script and Reno rehearsed his pitch and the next thing we know, he's blowing the doors off Evine! He put a bunch of food from the typical American diet in the blender, turned it on . . . and I'm not kidding you, the smell made us all want to vomit. It nearly made the on-camera talent vomit. You wonder why puke smells the way it smells? It's the crap most people eat! The smell was so bad it practically shut down taping for a while.

That was magic. That was the connection with the viewer. Then we said, "That's why you feel terrible. Here's how we're going to solve that problem." The solution, of course, was

Boku! It was a fantastic infomercial and the product is still one of the biggest sellers in its category today. *That* is framing.

What Do They *Need* to Know?

But there's a line here that I don't want you to cross as you learn to pitch: the line between the interesting storyteller and the windbag uncle who has everybody rolling their eyes and checking their watch. You know, the guy or gal who can't shut up and decides that everybody in the room *has* to know *every* detail about the new car or Cancun vacation. Details can be your best friend or worst enemy depending on how you use them, so here's the question you should be asking as you prepare your story: what does your audience need to know?

Remember, storytelling in the pitch is strategic. At each beat, you should be sharing facts and figures that serve your audience's interest. It doesn't matter what you want them to know. It only matters what they need to know to keep their interest and sway the outcome in your favor. Say you're in a competitive job interview for a job as a customer service rep, and you launch into a story about your last position. Each example should convey something about you that relates to the job you're after: you're patient, good with people, and a terrific problem solver, and so on. Anything else is extra baggage that you can toss over the side.

Under the Ether

This is the classic market pitchman's term for when all this is working. As I said in Chapter 2, having your audience "under the ether" means having them under your spell. I could always tell when I had my home show crowds under the ether, because I could move fifty people with a wave of my hand. They would be so caught up in the pitch and the show I was putting on that if I said, "Everyone take a step forward," they would all do it instantly, as one. That's your goal. Captivate and enthrall.

Here's a simple test to tell whether you've got your audience under the ether, one that works for one listener or a room of hundreds: *stop talking*. Pause and see what happens. An ordinary story is like pulling a sled uphill; when you stop providing the propulsive force, everything stops. You'll see people blink, check their phones, and look around. But a great story is like rowing a boat across calm water: if you stop rowing, the boat keeps gliding for a while. So pause. If your audience doesn't move and seems 100 percent with you, waiting breathlessly for the next word, you've got them under the ether.

When you do, you finish your story and then before they can recover, invite them to take action: "So, do you think all that makes me a perfect fit for this job or what?"

Other times this Pitch Power is like a power ring and utility belt rolled into one:

- **Hitting on somebody.** Lines rarely work. Honesty works better. But stories are magic. If you can get someone cute to sit still and listen to a really good story for a while, you've gotten past their natural barrier and improved your odds of scoring a number. But don't lie or exaggerate. It's more obvious than you think.
- **Commission sales.** Selling for your supper is rough work because the other party knows your income depends on how much you sell. That means their defenses are high, and a story can bring them down. Storytelling gets around sales resistance by engaging the listener in a narrative, not a sales pitch or list of features and benefits.

- **Coaching.** You might be coaching a sports team or coaching a team of subordinates at your workplace. You're still trying to teach people who may or may not want to learn. Rather than say, "Do this, then do that," share a story about someone who did things the right way and let that inspire your team. A lesson by example is always more effective than a lesson by lecture.

Story-Furthering Interlude

Public speaking might be a situation where superpowered storytelling can enthrall most people. Ramsey Jay Jr. knows that well. A Wall Street–trained finance professional, a Dartmouth College graduate named one of *Ebony* magazine's "30 Leaders of the Future" for 2007, and author of *Empowering Dreamers to Become Achievers*, he's a fast-rising star in the world of speaking. Among his many public-speaking highlights, in 2016 Ramsey delivered opening remarks at the White House at an evening musical celebration hosted by President Obama and First Lady Michelle Obama honoring the legendary Ray Charles. Additionally, he delivered the commencement address for the 105th graduating class at Dartmouth's Tuck School of Business, and he says that telling a gripping story is absolutely essential to reaching an audience.

"Storytelling allows me to paint a picture that's relevant to an audience," he says. "When you're speaking to a variety of audiences, you won't always have a story that's relevant to that audience but you can always tell a story that makes your point more personal and relatable. You take a concept that's universal and articulate it in a way that anyone can apply to their situation. Instead of just saying, 'If you have a dream, make it come true,' you say, 'Let me tell you about someone I think you can relate to.' You pivot from genetic to specific.

"One of my most effective stories, which I use to talk about bouncing back from disappointments, is about Michael Jordan when he was in high school," Jay continues. "He was a five-foot-nine sophomore and he tried out for the varsity team, and he was the last player cut from varsity. The twelfth player chosen was named Leroy Smith. But Jordan used that failure as his catalyzing fuel to work harder than ever between his sophomore and junior years, and we know the rest of the story. But no one knows who Leroy Smith is.

"When Jordan was inducted into the Hall of Fame, he thanked Phil Jackson, Scottie Pippen, and even coach Dean Smith from the University of North Carolina, but he also spent almost ninety seconds talking about Leroy Smith, who was in the audience," Jay goes on. "In his speech, Jordan said, 'The competitive fire that fueled me to work the next twenty years of my career was born out of the image of Leroy Smith that I kept in my mind throughout high school, college and pro career. He's the guy that lit that competitive fire.'

"You can imagine the impact that story has on all of my audiences, particularly those made up of high school students from disadvantaged backgrounds," Jay continues. "When I tell that story, they fact-check me on the spot. They go on the Internet then and there on their phones. Later, they'll email me and tell me they watched the speech on YouTube. I tell them that we all have that Leroy Smith moment, and we can come away from those disappointments in one of three ways: give up, aim lower, or use it to get better. Every time I tell that story, I hear half the audience going, 'Oh my God, I had my Leroy Smith moment and I didn't react like MJ.' That story drives home the truth, which is that while they can't be the next Jordan, they can rebound from failure like he did. Storytelling makes things like that immediately relatable to anyone."

Plot Twist!

My Thom Beers account shows that you don't need to tell a long story for it to be effective. In fact, extremely short stories can sometimes work to your advantage, because busy people like people who don't waste their time. Thom was and is a very big deal—not just the creator of *Deadliest Catch, Ice Road Truckers,* and *Ax Men*, but at the time the chairman and CEO of FremantleMedia North America—and he didn't have time for me to waste. Also, in this attention-deficit age, some people simply can't listen very long. So think of your story as a tweet instead of a post on Medium: tight, succinct, and strategic. However, even with that approach, you're going to run into some situations where a story is the wrong Pitch Power to roll out:

- **Any legal situation.** When you're talking to the police or an attorney, giving a deposition or in court, do not put on your storyteller hat. Any audience in the legal world is going to see a story as "spin." Take the approach of Sergeant Joe Friday from *Dragnet* (look it up on YouTube for pity's sake) and provide "just the facts" and nothing else.
- **When you're following somebody who won't shut up.** It's not your fault if the speaker who went on before you talked so much that he sucked every molecule of air from the room. But it is your fault if you go on and do the same thing. Being a superhero means being flexible, having long and short versions of your story or speech ready to go so you can adapt to the situation. If you're speaking or presenting after a chatterbox and you can see the audience is exhausted and irritated, play off it by saying something, like "Well, I'm going to be brief" (you'll probably get sarcastic, grateful applause) and go right into the pertinent

facts. If you gain the audience's trust you can always take questions at the end and tell your story then.

- **When the environment is distrustful.** I've talked with people in the venture capital world who've said that when an entrepreneur comes in to pitch them for money, they assume 90 percent of their story is bullshit. That's probably not the best environment to rest your pitch on your brilliant storytelling. Go to the facts and figures instead.
- **When the facts are overwhelmingly in your favor.** Remember, storytelling is all about getting the outcome you want: the sale, the job, the girl, or the standing ovation from folks who turn around and buy your book at the back of the room. But if you don't need a story, why use it? Let's say you're calling your credit card company to dispute a fraudulent charge that they won't remove from your account. You've got dates, times, phone records—massive amounts of data that prove beyond a shadow of a doubt that the charge is bogus. Why tell a story that's just going to waste time? Hit the customer service person with your facts and stick to them, and you'll probably get the result you want.

All that said, there probably aren't many situations in which a well-told, wisely edited, strategically constructed story won't help you in a big way. Do your research and know the environment and audience before you step in the door and adapt.

Training Montage

There are no shortcuts here: telling a great story that sells takes lots of practice. *Lots*. But not practice in a vacuum. Practice with other people who are willing to give you feedback. Find some good friends who you can torture with your stories

WHAT WOULD BILLY DO?

Billy Mays here! I loved telling stories when I was pitching, and the key for me was telling them with so much enthusiasm that it looked like I was having an awesome time just being there, even if I was telling the same story for the eight hundredth time . . . which I usually was! You're going to be in the same situation. If you have a handful of stories that work—like Sully's yarn about cleaning up after surfers in Hawaii—you're going to have to find a way to tell it again and again while looking like you're hearing it for the first time, just like your audience. So pretend. Yes, pretend. Pretend that while you're speaking, you're also hearing all this for the first time. Amp up the amazement, embarrassment, or "Can you believe that?" quality in your voice and manner. Use your hands to make points, something I did all the time. Most important, pay attention to how your listener is reacting to the story. If he or she is tickled or excited, let that make YOU tickled or excited. That's how you make the one-thousandth telling of a story—to quote a song from Foreigner—feel like the first time.

in return for food or beer, and then regale them with the time you MacGyvered a winning sales presentation with some quick computer graphics and a paper clip. At the end, ask for comments. Did you go too long? Did the story hold their interest? What were the high points? The weak points? How could you improve it? Obviously, you want people who will give you constructive feedback, not drinking buddies who'll make sarcastic jokes just to mess with you.

The second thing I recommend is to listen to as many storytellers as you can, good and bad. Check out *This American Life* on NPR or *The Moth* for terrific personal storytelling on the radio. View lots of TED talks, where you'll witness both incredibly compelling storytellers (Brené Brown is a winner) and some of the most pompous, self-indulgent crap on the planet. Go to see speakers in person so you can get a sense of an audience's body language when they're under the ether or bored senseless. Use what I've taught you to dissect winning speeches and figure out why they worked.

Talk to terrific storytellers and ask for their advice. These could include anyone who can really captivate a room, from college professors to ministers who give great sermons to commissioned salespeople who live and die based on their ability to persuade.

Finally, do your own prep work. What are the best, most interesting stories from your own life and career? How could you use them to get an audience under your spell or get a recruiter to offer you that job? Remember, storytellers are made, not born. Get to work.

SCENARIOS FOR USING THE "FACTS TELL, STORIES SELL" PITCH POWER

Q: *You finish telling what you think is an absolute crusher of a story: vivid, brief, and powerful. Then the listener accuses you of making it up. What do you do?*

A: That depends. If it *is* made up, then cop to it. "You got me. But I had you, didn't I? And if I can hold your attention with something I made up, imagine what I could do for your company!" If the story is real, then be ready for this. Have proof, like someone you can call on the spot to verify the account. That's a boss move.

Q: *You're in the middle of a story that's a crucial part of your pitch and the listener interrupts you, telling you to get on with it or something equally rude. Do you drop the story and try to gather your wits, move on with other material but come back to it, or explain that the story has a point and try to keep going?*

A: Cut to the chase, but stick to your story. If it's a critical part of your pitch, say something like "This is important, but I'll jump to the reason why."

Q: *You're in mid-story and your mind goes blank. Bluff your way through or own the mistake?*

A: Own it. Mistakes aren't a big deal as long as you can admit them and laugh about them. Blame it on a senior moment or too much Diet-Coke, get everybody laughing at you (and with you), and get back to it.

POWER NUMBER SEVEN

LOVE YOUR MISTAKES

Good for saving the day in live performances, speeches, client presentations, and any situation where humanizing yourself will help you connect with your audience.

WHEN WE LAST LEFT OUR HERO . . .

You were racking your brain for awesome stories you can use to captivate and disarm your audiences, and trying to figure out the best way to tell them. When you do, you're going to make mistakes. It's inevitable. But you can let those mistakes crush you or use them to make your pitch even more effective.

ORIGIN STORY

We're afraid of making mistakes. It's perfectly normal. But few people seem to appreciate how much power there is in embracing mistakes and using them to tickle someone's funny bone or make a human connection. I'll illustrate by telling you about one of the funniest things that's ever happened to me.

When I was a kid in England I had an old piece of shit Mini, and I loved it. Then when I was living in the United States an all-new version of the Mini became available, and I was delighted. My then-wife Randi had a Beetle and didn't like it. I said, "Why don't we go look at Minis? They're really cool. They suit your personality." So we drove to Ferman BMW and the salesman said, "You want to go for a test drive?" Of course we did. Then he offered to drive, which was odd. He said, "I'll drive out and you can drive back." Okay.

We got in the Mini, with Randi in the back, and he said, "This has got some power. You should put seat belts on." We did, and then this guy spun the wheels like he was auditioning for *The Italian Job*. He laid rubber taking off—we were still in the dealership lot, mind you—and he tore around a corner like Mario Andretti, and I've driven with Mario. It was terrifying.

Well, the parking lot was cambered, like the back of a whale, and he hit that slope going about eighty miles an hour. We caught air and Randi was screaming in the back for him to stop. Then we landed on the tarmac and immediately spun sideways, skidding through an adjacent parking lot. I was thinking, *I'm going to* die. I was a second from reaching over and punching this guy in the face when—you know those big lights in the middle of parking lots with high curbstones around them? We smacked into one, hard, bending the front wheel under the car horizontally. We had snapped the axle!

So we sat there, shaking, like you do, taking inventory. Are we safe? Are we alive? Randi was sobbing and I was furious. I screamed, "What the fuck are you doing?"

He said, "It's not that bad, it's not that bad."

"Not that bad? This car is not even drivable and you're an asshole." I let Randi out of the back and we walked back to the dealership, shaken. All the while, I was waiting for Ashton Kutcher to come out and tell me I'd been punked. We got back to the dealership, walked in, and Aaron, the sales manager, took a look at us and said, "What happened?"

I was still seething. "Your guy ran into the curb. He almost killed us."

Aaron said, "That's not very good, is it?"

Really? That's all you have to say? "Before I leave this dealership," I said, "I want that guy to be not working here anymore. He shouldn't be allowed to take people on test drives. He's dangerous." They called the manager and he said, "I wouldn't be that worried about it."

I glared at him. "We nearly died."

His response was to pretend the whole thing was just some lark, some misunderstanding, and to try and offer me some piss-poor discount on a Mini. You know what? I might have actually bought the car—*if* they'd had the balls to own the mistake, fire the salesman, and use the situation to pitch me. If Aaron had laughed and said, "Sorry you almost died, but how about that power? Can you imagine a car that handles like that on a mountain road?" I would've respected the chutzpah and probably said, "Yeah, dude, it was fast."

They would've had to knock a massive amount off the price of the car for, you know, almost killing us, but I would have bought the car. But they blew it. They could've had a story and a customer, but they wimped out and we walked. We went and bought a Range Rover instead.

You Know, They Know

They say it's not the crime, it's the cover-up. Right? Absolutely true, and yet it amazes me how many people screw up during a pitch, think no one will notice, and then pretend it didn't happen. That does. Not. Work. Trust me, everyone saw what just happened, and it's a moment of truth. Moments of truth are when you show who you are and reveal your character. If you're a pitching superhero, you use mistakes to make yourself accessible, make people laugh, and break the force field a little more.

A few years ago, there was a host on a shopping network. Great gal. One day, she was live, selling these plates that were supposedly unbreakable. Yeah, you know where this is going, don't you? She opened up her pitch and went on and on about these wonderful plates that you could drop and abuse and they would not break. And then she dropped one.

You know those moments when things go into slow motion? That was one of them. You could see the plate flipping end over end, her surprised face, the light glistening off the product. And then it hit the floor—and shattered into a million pieces. It was one of those perfect fuck-ups, like the perfect storm of home shopping. But, God love her, she laughed about it and said something like "Well, it's a good thing these plates come with a money-back guarantee!" and kept on going. It was terrific.

We're so terrified of mistakes that we like to pretend they don't happen. When we do that we lose the chance to do things that can really earn warmth and love from an audience and even get them on our side: admit we're human, solve problems, and prove that we are who we say we are when things are going well. That's a lost opportunity, and I'm going to tell you how to take advantage of it instead.

THE REVEAL

It's a reflex to back away from mistakes as fast you'd back away from a rattlesnake that you found on a hiking trail. But if you're going to be a superpowered pitching pro, you actually need to do the opposite. Because when you're trying to sell, persuade, or captivate anyone in any situation, you can be absolutely, 100 percent certain that three things will happen:

1. You will be nervous.
2. You will screw it up at least once, no matter how well prepared you are.
3. Somebody in the room will notice the first two, even if it's just you.

When those things happen, you also have three choices:

1. If you're the only one who noticed, keep going as though nothing has happened.
2. If your nerves or flub are so obvious that the other party can't help but notice, pretend nothing happened and push on.
3. Acknowledge your slipup and use it to your advantage.

If you've ever done drama, your teacher or director probably told you, "If you make a mistake, keep going! The audience won't know unless you stop and say, 'Oh, shit!'" For the most part, that's true, though I do wonder how thick a theatergoer would have to be not to pick up the mistake in "To be or not to be, that is the questlove." But I digress. The point is, pitching isn't theater. You might have an audience of one, up close and very personal. They're likely to pick up on your mistakes, especially if this isn't their first rodeo. A venture capital firm that's watched thousands of entrepreneurs pass through with their pitch decks asking for money has probably seen every blunder a group of twenty-four-year-old Stanford grads can make—and all the ways they can try to cover them up, too.

So don't try to fool your audience. Mistakes can be your best friends, so treat them that way. In other words . . .

LOVE YOUR MISTAKES

Using this Pitch Power means reprogramming that part of your brain that screams, *Shit! I forgot what I was going to say! Activate Distraction Mode!* No. Stop. Don't act cool, cover up, or anything else. As triathlete Chris "Macca" McCormack (who I mentioned earlier) says about that moment when he starts to suffer in a race, "Embrace the suck." Own up to your mistake. Admit you're nervous. Laugh about it. Get the other people laughing about it. Because guess what: we've all been there. We've all screwed up, dropped the meat in the dirt, and flubbed our lines. Love your mistakes and you'll get them laughing *with* you, not *at* you.

Anatomy of a Superpower

When I talk with young people who are trying to learn how to pitch, one of the most common misconceptions is that being a great persuader or pitchman means not making mistakes: training the risk out of your presentation. But nothing could be further from the truth, for two reasons. First, you won't learn Pitch Powers unless you're willing to step onto the stage and risk looking like an idiot, like I did on the first day I pitched the car washer in the market in Devon. The only way you'll learn is to step into the lion's den, make mistakes, recover from them, and develop your tools. It's that way with anything you do, really. If you don't want to make mistakes, you'll hide in your house eating Hot Pockets and watching Netflix and never come out. Don't do that.

THE PERSUADER!

We've talked about confidence a lot, and the Persuader knows that one of the ways a real pitching superhero shows confidence is by refusing to be thrown by a mistake.

"When I'm trying to persuade someone in a tight situation," says the Persuader, "and I botch a line or forget something I was going to say, I break the fourth wall and actually comment on my own error. I'll say something like 'Well, I didn't exactly stick the landing on that joke, did I?' That tells my listener that I'm so confident that I can poke fun at my own errors, which not everyone can do. That's black-belt pitching skill."

So if you accept mistakes as an integral part of pitching, then the obvious question is, "Okay, Sully, if I'm going to make mistakes, how do I make sure that I get as much out of them as possible?" Fair question. Here are six ways to do that:

1. Make 'em loud. They say, "Go big or go home," and that includes your errors. Loud mistakes are the ones you make because you took a big, big risk with a potentially huge payoff. In finance, the bigger the potential return on your investment, the bigger the potential risk that you might lose it all, right? It's the same in pitching. Sure, you can play it safe and ask out the plain-looking guy or gal who you know will say yes because they're grateful for the attention, or you could risk getting shot down and ask out the supermodel over there. You might have to do the walk of shame—or you might just shock your mates and end up with the number of the hottest person at the club! Loud mistakes have the biggest possible payoff.

This is where it helps to not mind looking a little like a fool. As you already know, I don't. I'm willing to make an ass of myself to improve my odds in a situation. For example, about eighteen years ago there was a reality show called the *Eco-Challenge*, which was Mark Burnett's first show before he did *Survivor* and *The Apprentice*. I'm a huge fan of Mark's and I really wanted to be on *Eco-Challenge*—and I have been known to do crazy shit to meet people.

First, I watched all the episodes, and then sat down with my buddy in Tampa and I said, "I'm going to do the *Eco-Challenge* next year." He started laughing at me, so I went on the website and filled out the application. It was funny: I had even assembled a team of four, but I hadn't told the other people yet! Or it *would've* been funny if I'd gotten in, but I got an email back from a lady named Lisa Hennessy, who said that they didn't have room for more teams but did have some individual spots left. If I wanted to do an individual application, she'd try and put me with a team.

I looked at the application for individuals and started sweating. You basically had to be superhuman: done an Ironman triathlon, swum across the English Channel, climbed a mountain, traversed a continent solo on a bike, or something like that. I didn't have any of those credentials. So I put on my Persuader mask and thought, *How am I going to make my application stand out?*

I decided the only shot I had was to make it funny. After all, it was a TV show, which means it had to be entertaining. I had no problem being the class clown if it got me what I wanted. So I got a box and put my Boy Scout knot-tying certificates in there. I got pictures of me as a kid, my report card, and pictures of crazy things I did when I was ten or twelve years old. Then I filled the box up with "As Seen on TV" swag: Turbie Twists, a box of OxiClean, Sonic Scrubbers, every product I had ever sold on television. I put them all in a box that was so heavy I could barely lift it, and shipped it to the production offices.

It was a crazy long shot, but I knew there would be ten thousand envelopes in there and one massive box. It would stand out. The next month, I got a phone call from Lisa telling me they had chosen me for *Eco-Challenge* because mine was the funniest application they ever received. They had chosen me because I had made them laugh, not because of my credentials. Everyone in the office was wearing a Turbie Twist, this towel-like head wrap that looks like a turban. The whole thing cost me a hundred bucks, but I got on the show, met Mark Burnett, and made a ton of friends. If I hadn't been willing to get creative, look stupid, and flop miserably, none of it would've happened.

2. Frontload your nervousness. People love when you can analyze your own nerves and cop to them, because we've all been there. There's nothing wrong with going in and admitting to people that you're jittery. I have been very honest in some pitching situations about how nervous I was, and that changes expectations in your favor. Instantly, you go from someone expected to deliver a flawless performance to someone working to overcome fear. Go as far as to say, "I am a nervous wreck right now, but I am going to do my best." Already, you've won the crowd by being honest and vulnerable.

Being self-deprecating and owning your flaws is another way to do this. Comedians are great at it. If a comedian is an alcoholic, she'll use it. If she got teased in school, she'll bring it up in her act. Don't pretend you're perfect. Be flawed. If you have a strange speaking voice, get out in front of it by saying, "I know my voice is high pitched, but don't worry, I supply all my own helium" or some such line. People will laugh with you if you can make fun of yourself. Don't take yourself too seriously.

3. Plan your comebacks. Later, in the Training Montage section, I'm going to talk about the virtues of watching stand-up comedians to learn about mistakes. They're brilliant at leveraging them. Hecklers are a common way that things can go awry in a comedy club, and good comics plan how to handle hecklers. Many years ago, when Steve Martin was a stand-up star, he had a terrific comeback when someone got rowdy at his shows. He would muse, "Yeah, I remember when I had my first beer . . ." The audience always howled at his soft mocking of the usually drunk heckler. That was a planned comeback, and you should have some idea of what you'll say and do if you spill a glass of water, forget details from a story, or accidentally drop a "fuck" or "shit." Leave yourself room to improvise, which you will get better at the more you pitch. But plan and rehearse some responses. If nothing else, they'll be a relaxing security blanket.

4. Breathe. When you mess up, don't panic and rush to cover up your mistake. Stop. Slow down. Breathe. Take a pause. Find a moment. When you pause, the audience pauses with that pause. They will feel the gap. Even though it may feel like an uncomfortably long silence, you are allowing your audience to process what just happened: you're nervous, you made an error, now you're regaining your composure. Believe me, you will earn more respect from the people listening by taking a moment to gather yourself, which is what a professional would do, instead of rushing on like nothing happened.

5. Get them on your side. You've heard about that old trick for nervous public speakers where you're supposed to imagine the audience members in their underwear. The idea is that we're all human. You could just as easily imagine the audience spilling coffee or having a PowerPoint crash in mid-presentation, because there's no one you can pitch who hasn't made mistakes that seemed *catastrophic* at the time. But you know what's funny? If you ask them about those same mistakes today, they'll laugh. Misfortunes make the best stories!

So, when you trip over your tongue, say, "Well, I blew that punchline. Who hasn't done that, right?" Odds are you'll get smiles, maybe a few shared stories, and some priceless common ground.

6. Find a scapegoat. I don't mean someone to blame for real, but a comic sense. If you're pitching as a group or team—soliciting venture capital, to go back to my earlier example—designate one person as the clown or jester: the one who gets the blame in a tongue-in-cheek way when something goes wrong.

I did this all the time pitching in street markets and in home shows. Inevitably, some small piece of the Smart Mop or Amazing Washmatik would break at some point, because in doing fifty pitches a day we tortured those products. So I'd pull the mop out of my bucket and there'd be no mop, just a stick. Guess who knew? Nobody. I'd have a hundred people in front of me and without missing a beat I'd say, "Ladies and gentlemen, I'll bet you think the mop I'm using is the only one that works, right? You've been to these fairs before and seen a lot of bogus products. Well, I'm going to prove that every one of these mops is as good as the next. Pick one and I'll do my demo with it." Then I would casually set the broken mop aside and keep going.

If a mistake was too obvious to miss, however, I always had a—well, in America they call him a prat; in England, he's the schlepper. Anyway, I always had a whipping boy who couldn't do anything right, was to blame for whatever went wrong, and who I used to scream at all the time. If I was selling a vegetable slicer, I could turn my back to my crowd and yell, "Where the heck is my tomato?" and the people would be howling. Try turning your back on your audience anywhere else and see how many of them leave.

It was a two-man comedy act, and the prat was my court jester. I announced us by saying things like "We're the Sym-

INCOMPETENT SIDEKICK: PERFECTO THE PERFECTIONIST

Perfecto is a real pain in the ass. He never seems to understand that while you should practice in order to get your pitch theoretically perfect, it will never be perfect in practice. You will slip up. But Perfecto will freak out when you do: panic, freeze, ask to start over, all those awful things. Keep him out of the room, theater, lecture hall, or bar—wherever you're pitching. The only way a mistake can really trip you up is if you let him turn it into the Apocalypse. We all mess up. Heck, even President Obama did it when he compared his bad bowling to the Special Olympics. He made a sincere apology and moved on. Do the same.

bolics! I'm Sim, and he's Bollocks!" or "I'm Anthony the Magnificent, and this is my partner . . . John." I was always riding his ass and the crowd loved it because he was useless. If something broke or I didn't have a mop head or chamois, I would turn around and berate this poor bloke, then turn back to the crowd and say, "You just can't get good help anymore!" They would be wetting their pants while he scrambled and fumbled to get me what I needed. It was perfect.

Remember, the people you're persuading are just people. Make them laugh or touch their empathy and you're one big step closer to getting what you want. Don't fear mistakes; treat them as one more tool.

WITH GREAT POWER COMES GREAT RESPONSIBILITY

I know, I know. That's hard to do. We're programmed in our society to cover up our mistakes and fear failure more than death. But here's a reality that makes it easier to embrace mistakes: most people are going to want you to succeed. I've already talked about what I call the "ace to the top of the deck" effect, which is where the person conducting auditions, interviewing job applicants, or getting hit on over and over at the bar is dying for someone to step up and be *amazing* so the whole thing can be over. But this isn't that.

This is simpler. Most people are decent and they want to see everyone do well. That's why audition reality shows like *The Voice* are incredibly popular: people are putting it all on the line, risking national humiliation, and we really, really want to see them do well. It's human nature, written into the DNA. We're altruistic. If you ask for help, people will try to help you. If you watch *Shark Tank*, you see a lot of people crash and burn and cry, but you *want* to see people succeed. So do the hosts. People you pitch will mostly be the same way. They know that you are powering through the same kind of crushing anxiety that they would be feeling if they were in your shoes. That's nearly universal. You've got to be a sociopath to really want to watch somebody fail.

That was the nature of Billy's and my reality show, *Pitchmen*. These inexperienced entrepreneurs would come to us with products and pitch us on them, and of course they would be terrible at it. But we would see something in one of them that stood out, and we'd put them on the show and teach them how to pitch. They'd still be awful at it, and they would make mistakes and get better, but by the time we took them out to pitch product development or marketing companies, they would still be as green as month-old ground beef.

Didn't matter. Why? Because we knew that even the hardened direct-response pros they'd be pitching would respect the hell of the fact that they were out there doing it at all. They would be forgiving of mistakes and awkwardness because they wanted them to be successful. Never forget that and it will help to win in some important situations:

- **Meeting someone intimidating.** I've done some stupid stuff to meet famous people, but the best advice is the simplest. *Do it*. Don't psych yourself out. Case in point: my mum loves Mick Fleetwood of Fleetwood Mac, but he famously doesn't take photos with fans. Challenge accepted. Fleetwood Mac were in concert in Tampa and I was with the tour manager, Bobby Hare, a good friend. My mum and I had backstage passes and we were leaving through the rear parking lot when I saw four Cadillac Escalades, which is what the band members ride in instead of a tour bus. I said, "Let's wait here. The band's going to come out any second. Let's see what will happen."

The next moment, I saw Mick Fleetwood walk out. Mum whispers, "Fuck me, it's Mick Fleetwood."

I said, "Let's go and ask him for a picture," but she got scared.

"No, no, I can't, I can't." But I took her by the hand and pulled her along. I was going to pitch my way into a picture for her. Understand, this was like walking up to the president, with security guards on high alert; I didn't want to get Tased. So I looked at Bobby, and then at Mick. Bobby gave Mick a little nod and wink to say, *It's okay,* and I knew we were in.

I said, "Mum, just go and ask him. You're seventy-two years old; he's not going to be mean to you." I pushed her forward and said, "Mr. Fleetwood, say hi to my mum." She got the picture, looking like she'd died, gone to heaven, and won the lottery at the same time. Now she has a photo of her and Mick Fleetwood on her fridge.

- **Following a dull speaker.** If the person speaking before you at an event is a crashing bore, your audience might be begging for you to put them out of their misery. Instead, be their hero by making fun of yourself or talking about your own mistakes. You'll change the atmosphere in the room and win their devotion.

- **Most social situations.** From dating to parties to nights out, social occasions are full of people trying to look effortlessly cool, flawless, and successful. If you're the person who wears mismatched socks, mispronounces the name of the wine, or drips salsa on your shirt, so what? Make light of it. Make a joke out of it. Get into it. You'll be the entertaining one everybody else wants to hang around with.

Story-Furthering Interlude

Like most stand-up comedians, Carole Montgomery knows the value of embracing a flub and turning a heckler's comment into a side-splitting quip. She's been doing stand-up since the mid-1980s, first in New York (where she now lives), later in Los Angeles, and for years as a headliner in Las Vegas at hotels like the Riviera and the Luxor. She talked to me about the times she's dealt with unexpected reverses in her shows and turned them to her advantage.

"Twenty-five years ago, I was working the Pittsburgh Funny Bone when, in the middle of my act, all of a sudden the lights went out," she says. "I mean, it was pitch black. The thing was, the club was in a mall and without electricity, nobody could leave. Well, I have a loud voice, so I told people to relax and they did. But I had to keep doing my act to keep them relaxed, and a lot of my stuff depended on my facial expressions, so they needed to be able to see my face. I had the emcee go into the balcony with a flashlight and shine it on me, and I did my whole act like that. I didn't change my act a bit, and we got through it.

"Another time in Vegas," Carole continues, "I was on stage doing my act and saw somebody in the second row grab their chest. I made a joke of it, because that's what you did but this woman really had a heart attack. Then a minute later, the woman next to her had a heart attack. We had to stop the show and call the paramedics. What could I do? I said, 'The owner will return your money, but when we get these people to the hospital, if you want to stay, I'll do the show for you guys.' It took maybe forty-five minutes to get them out of the room, and then I went back on stage and did my full show—and hardly anybody left!

"You have to roll with the punches," she concludes. "I worked Vegas for ten years, and you learn how to be a crowd comic, the one warming up the audience. You go out and talk to people; you don't know what they're going to say and you don't even know if they speak English. But once you know you can make them laugh, the rest is easy."

Plot Twist!

All this good advice aside, there are a few situations where mistakes will really undermine you. Anytime you're coming into a situation where the audience perceives you as an expert—something legal, medical, financial, technical—mistakes will just damage your credibility. It's also bad when you make a mistake at what you're there to convince your listeners you're good at. For instance, if you're pitching a client on your firm's graphic design services, don't come to a meeting with sample company logos where the company name is misspelled.

Finally, mistakes are most damaging when you're doing something where near-flawless preparation is *part* of what you're expected to deliver. If you audition for a play, you're expected to know the audition scene or song backwards and forwards. A mistake won't be taken as a charming sign that you're human, but as a warning sign that you're not capable of preparing like a professional.

Know the small number of situations where mistakes will ruin you and when faced with them, prepare and rehearse until you're sick of the routine, then do it again.

WHAT WOULD BILLY DO?

Billy Mays here! I'd love to talk about my mistakes, but I never made any! Kidding! Seriously, whether I was on HSN or doing TV commercials or doing a live event, I botched things all the time. The key was that I kept going. I knew that people loved watching a celebrity like me blow a line, drop a product, or stumble over my words, and that they would tell their friends about it later: "Hey, I saw that OxiClean guy almost fall on his face!" Great, as long as they're entertained. But that meant I could get away with all but the worst screw-ups because the audience enjoyed them, so I didn't worry about them. That let me dial my intensity up to eleven and put on a great show!

Training Montage

There are two sides to training to hone this Pitch Power: seeing how other people handle mistakes and getting comfortable leveraging your own. For the first one, there are two can't-miss venues. First, go anywhere you can find pitchmen on microphones pitching products: Costco, a weekend home show, a flea market, or a county fair. Stop and watch, even if you don't buy (though that drives us crazy). See how the pitchman deals with dropping stuff, messes, or rude audience members. Remember that 90 percent of his responses are planned and honed over time until they look seamless. If you're really brave, take him aside after his shift and ask him how he handles mistakes.

Second, watch tons of live stand-up and improv comedy. Go to clubs and "comedy sports" events and see how comics turn heckling, bad improv lines, and things like equipment failures into comedy gold. You'll see that it's mostly about acknowledging that the blunder happened, adopting a kind of eye-rolling "doesn't this happen to everyone" attitude, and cracking wise.

What about getting comfortable with your own mistakes? For that, you have to learn by doing and take some risks, and the perfect way to do it is to try your own hand at comedy. Take a stand-up class, tell a few jokes at an open-mic night, or take an improv class. Improv is especially useful, not only because it forces you to think on your feet, but because it's unpredictable.

My other suggestion is a repeat from the chapter on breaching the force field: try giving something away or pitching to the public in another situation where you have little or no control, like running a lemonade stand with your kids or offering car washes for charity. Try that sort of thing for hours and you'll run the gamut of mistakes and embarrassments: rude customers, equipment breakdowns, lost supplies, spills, forgotten patter, even bad weather. You'll be forced to think fast, keep your cool, maintain a smile, and turn that sow's ear into a silk purse by making people laugh.

SCENARIOS FOR USING THE "LOVE YOUR MISTAKES" PITCH POWER

Q: *You're pitching and you forget a story or fact. You admit it, laugh at yourself, and look up to see nobody laughing with you. Do you comment on the lack of humor in the room or get serious and keep going?*

A: Let it go and get on with it. One thing you can't do is MAKE people have a sense of humor. Some don't.

Q: *You're pitching and trip up, but you make it work for you by making fun of yourself. Great, except that now, someone in your audience decides to seize the floor by going on about how he made this ridiculous mistake this one time. Shut him down to get back control of the situation, or let him go and play off what he says?*

A: Unless you're on a tight schedule, work with your audience. Be transparent about not letting the other person drone on ("Hey, Joe, that's hilarious but I've got to bore the pants off of three other companies before noon") but be ready to jump in and use his/her story as an example of why mistakes aren't fatal or something like that.

Q: *You've said or done something tasteless and your audience looks appalled. Can this pitch be saved, or is it bound for the lava pit?*

A: Depends on the audience. I like the line from *Amadeus*, after Mozart swears in front of the emperor: "I'm a vulgar man. But I assure you my music is not." Own it, apologize, wink at the ones who secretly liked it, and pivot.

POWER NUMBER EIGHT

PUSH BACK

Good for saving the day in tough sales meetings, grueling job interviews, proposal presentations to hard-ass prospects, situations where you're waiting on demanding diners.

WHEN WE LAST LEFT OUR HERO . . .

You were steeling your nerves to turn inevitable blunders and slipups into moments of winning, charming vulnerability, and humanity. Well, enough of that. It's time to get tough and learn how not to take no for an answer.

ORIGIN STORY

In 2016, I had the chance to meet with Liz Smith, CEO of Bloomin' Brands, the company that runs big chain restaurants like Outback Steakhouse and Bonefish Grill. They're a multi-billion-dollar company and it would've been a major coup to get their TV advertising business for Sullivan Productions. At the time, their stock price was relatively low, and I wasn't seeing a lot of good television advertising for their brands, so I thought I had something to offer. Plus, Liz is good friends with Mindy Grossman, the CEO of HSN, and the CEO of Church & Dwight, Jim Craigie, was on the board of Bloomin' Brands. I used those connections to get a meeting to pitch her, which was pretty convenient since she lives six houses down the street from me.

I knew it would be a challenging meeting. Liz is the powerful CEO of a major publicly traded company, and she's tough, smart, demanding and shrewd. I ended up not doing business with her company at the time, but that was my choice. That I had the opportunity at all was a direct result of pushing back and flipping the script on her.

I felt pretty good about the meeting before it started, so I didn't go in armed with a pitch deck or a presentation. I figured I would use my Pitch Powers to start a conversation and feel out the situation. I would spend fifteen to twenty minutes making my case and find out her level of interest. The way I saw it, our work had helped grow Nutrisystem and Church & Dwight, the parent company of OxiClean, and I thought we could do something good for this restaurant behemoth.

I walked into Liz's Tampa office and we started talking about the neighborhood and how it had changed. Then I asked her about the possibility of working together, and she said, "There's no way that Outback is going to work with you. We don't do cleaning products. We don't do direct response. We don't do cheesy infomercials." Just like that, she threw my entire business under the bus.

I was nonplussed—for about three seconds. I'm a veteran pitchman, and we don't rattle easily. Instead of backing off, which is what I think she expected, I pushed harder. I leaned into the conversation and said, "Liz, I disagree with you. I think you absolutely should look at working with us. I don't see you in any media right now that is getting any attention. I don't think your stock price is where you'd like it to be, and I think across Bonefish, Outback, and your other brands, there's something we can do that won't cost you a fortune."

Before she could reply, I added, "By the way, I'm not asking to be your agency of record. I'm not asking for a giant contract. I would just like to sit down with someone in your marketing team to see if there's something we can do." Then I went for the power close: "I wouldn't waste my time driving over the bridge to sit in a meeting with you, and waste *your* time, unless I thought I could help you. I'm not stupid." I also knew from my research (preparation!) that Liz had held a senior position at Avon Cosmetics, so she knew plenty about my line of work.

The Bonefish Project

I think Liz was a little surprised. But pushing back broke the ice. She saw that I was serious and passionate. She called her chief marketing officer into the meeting, and as it happened, his background was at Burger King. *Jackpot*. Burger King is all about direct response: two burgers for a buck, two Whoppers for fifty cents. They're the direct-response kings of fast food.

I speak fluent direct response, so the CMO and I started vibing like two musicians in a rehearsal space. Finally, Liz said, "I'm really worried about putting you two in a room together because I think something may come of this." I had made a big pushback, and by pushing back I had ended up face to face with the guy I needed to be talking to anyway.

I asked the CMO how Bloomin' Brands did its advertising, and when he told me, it was clear they had been following a traditional model that was very expensive. I told him there was another way, and that's how I ended up with the entire Bonefish Grill marketing team at my office, talking shop and brainstorming. After a while, we hit on a perfect test project: Bonefish had an annual sales meeting coming up and my team would shoot a green-screen sales video for them.

Well, best-laid plans and all that. For several reasons, I decided that the timing wasn't right to work with Bloomin' Brands, and I told them I would wait for another opportunity. However, by leaning in and pushing back in my meeting with Liz—something that took balls and a real belief in what I could offer—I laid the groundwork for a solid relationship. Eventually, it paid off: Bloomin' Brands has become a Sullivan Productions client.

THE REVEAL

The Pitch Powers I've taught you work really well. I'm living proof of that. But they don't work every time you use them. That makes sense, right? This isn't mind control; it's persuasion. So every now and then, even if you prepare and command everyone's attention and tell a brilliant story, the person across the table from you is going to get that "somebody just pissed in my Weetabix" purse to their lips and let you know they're not buying what you're selling. At that moment, you have to make a decision: give up or . . .

PUSH BACK

Not every pitch will go the way you hope. Sometimes, the client says, "The other company has a lot more experience than yours. Why should we hire you?" The spokesman for the party of twelve who ran you ragged all night says, "You know, I know we drank it all, but the wine really wasn't that great. I think you should comp it." The attractive person you've bought three drinks for says, "You're very nice, but you're really not my type." Ouch. Sudden reversals hurt, but pitching superheroes

THE PERSUADER!

Pushing back means catching the other party by surprise. That means completely defying their expectations from the outset, right? Wrong.

The Persuader says: "It's better to know your audience's expectations and meet them in the beginning—to look like you're playing by their rules. After all, that's how they'll judge you. For example, if you're going to a meeting at an ebony and marble office tower on Park Avenue, you don't go in jeans no matter how badly you want to play the part of the rebellious creative type. You wear a suit. You let them know you get it, that you can meet them halfway. But you have an ace—an idea or a change of tone—in your back pocket, ready to play when you need it."

don't quit in the face of adversity. They push back, flipping the script on the other person by saying or doing something he or she doesn't expect.

Remember something that's easy to forget about most pitching situations: the person you're talking to probably wants to be convinced that you're the solution to their problems. The person interviewing applicants wants to hire the best candidate. The woman at the bar really would love to be asked out by someone terrific. Did you know Jennifer Lawrence—gorgeous, lovable, Oscar-winning Jennifer Lawrence—says she rarely gets asked out because guys all think she's out of their league? It's true. Sometimes, pushback is a test to see how badly you want what you're pitching for. Hunger matters. When the other person pushes, they may want you to push back to see what you're made of. Show them.

Anatomy of a Superpower

Remember Susan Boyle? If you don't know who she is, google "Susan Boyle Britain's Got Talent" and watch the YouTube clip that comes up. I'll wait.

[hums an aimless tune somewhat impatiently]

Didn't that leave you gobsmacked? In case you didn't watch the clip because you're on a plane or didn't feel like getting off the couch, I'll recap. In 2009, Susan Boyle was one of hundreds of people to audition for *Britain's Got Talent*, sort of the English version of *American Idol* or *The Voice*. But she stands out not only because of her talent but because of how everyone reacted to her. She was this dumpy, homely woman from this small Scottish village who strutted on stage and told everyone that she aspired to be like musical theater legend Elaine Paige. The cameras showed audience members grimacing at Susan's appearance and cheek at comparing herself to a West End star. The judges were cynical, too.

Then Susan opened her mouth and a soaring rendition of "I Dreamed a Dream" from *Les Miserables* came out. Everyone's jaw fell open. Even Simon Cowell, who can come off pretty smug on the show, was flabbergasted. The audience went nuts and when she finished, gave her a standing ovation. Susan went on to take second place that season, but got a recording contract and since then, has released multiple albums and has a legitimate career as a vocalist. It's really an inspiring story.

It very easily could have gone the other way. Plenty of people would've felt the doubt and animosity from the audience, gotten stage fright, and not been able to sing a note. This was the first time that Susan had sung since the death of her mother, and nobody would have blamed her if she'd been so intimidated by the giant audience and the judges that she'd walked right off stage. But she had the courage to push back.

A lot of people are afraid to do that. They get *I can't do it* stuck on repeat in their heads. *Yes, you can. Let them know. Let them have it.* That's the pitchman's inner monologue.

Confidence and a bit of fearlessness are critical for flipping the script. You can have all the plans in the world, but if you lose your nerve you'll wind up slinking from the room like a kicked cat. You see this all the time on *Shark Tank*. The aspiring entrepreneur is sitting in front of Mark Cuban and Barbara Corcoran, who knock down their idea. Then the music goes "duh-DUM." Sometimes, you see the person who's pitching take a breath and then push back. Those are the people who get funded.

There's nothing wrong with pushing back and flipping the script. You have to view it as an opportunity. You have to be prepared for resistance, for someone to say, "We don't want you; this is a shitty idea." Pushback is a great opportunity for you to show what you're really made of. When you have the balls to swallow that bitter pill and say, "You know what, I think you're wrong, and here's why . . ." you become an underdog. Anyone who's successful *loves* tenacity. When I'm trying to usher you out of the room and you're not leaving, you have my attention.

How many deals have gotten done after a powerful person said no, expecting the other person to walk away meekly with their hat in hand, but instead the other person stands firm. You get some uncomfortable silences, because when you're the one who flips the script, you're not playing by the rules. You're making them hear you out and tipping the power balance in the room in your direction. Flipping the script and refusing to budge when you get pushback is a boss move that earns respect.

Loading the Dice

However, in my experience a high percentage of people turn around with their head down and walk out of the room when they get rejected. I think they do that not because they don't "want it" more than the other guy or because they're cowards, but because they honestly thought when they stepped in the room that everything would go according to plan.

Pitchman fact: nothing ever goes *exactly* according to plan. You're dealing with human beings, which means politics and agendas that you know nothing about. Your product demo might fail. You might have spinach in your teeth. Something always goes sideways. You should go into any pitching situation assuming that somewhere along the line, your Pitch Power is going to fail you and you're going to be left standing there holding a yet to be determined body part in your hand.

That's where the "I won't take no for an answer" mentality is crucial. You really have to believe in yourself and what you have to offer. But there's also a smart way to approach the potential of failure: by reducing the odds that it will happen. I call that "loading the dice." Basically, you do whatever you can do to tilt the playing field in your favor before you ever step into the pitching situation. If you're planning to ask someone for a date, you might have a friend talk to him about all your great qualities first. If you're going to start looking for a new job, you might publish a few smart articles about your field on your blog. Loading the dice can even be as basic as finding out the name of the venture capitalist you'll be meeting with next week, finding out where he works out, and just "happening" to be there and introducing yourself. Anything you can do to make the other party see you in a more positive light, do. Because while pushing back against rejection is great, the best rejection is the kind that doesn't happen.

Here's an example of what I mean. It was a few weeks after Billy Mays had died back in 2009 and I was out for a run near my home in Tampa. I was still really broken up, because Billy wasn't just my partner but my best pal. So, in the middle of my run, this kid maybe ten or eleven years old rides up to me on his bike.

"Hey, man, you're the pitchman, aren't you?"

What the hell? I kept running but I was polite. "Yeah."

"Hey, I really loved your TV show."

"Thanks."

"I'm really sorry about Billy Mays."

That touched me. "Thanks, kid." Then he just took off on his bike. I was floored. What kid just comes up to a stranger on a bicycle and announces himself, super confident like that?

A week later, the same kid showed up at my front doorstep selling magazines. I opened the door and he stepped back and said, "Hi, Mr. Sullivan."

It didn't register, so I said, "Do I know you?"

"Yeah, I'm the kid on the bike. John Domenici." Now I remembered. But did he want an autograph?

"What do you want?"

"I got some magazines." What guts and smarts! He was selling them for Boy Scout troop or something, so I let him in. Let me tell you, this kid put on a pitching clinic. He knew every single magazine, had the prices down, and what you would pay if you bought three or four subscriptions. He wasn't good; he was *great*. He figured out what I liked, did the math in his head on the spot, and hit me for $100. I couldn't say no to him.

INCOMPETENT SIDEKICK: THE UNDERMINER

Before you even start your pitch, this joker will sabotage it by apologizing for what you're pitching. He'll say things like "I know I don't have the qualifications you listed in your ad" or "My price might be a bit higher than the other vendors you've talked to, but . . ." He'll fill the room with negative energy, take the starch right out of your pitch, and have the other party thinking, *What a wuss!* Don't even let the Underminer in. Whatever you're pitching—a product, a company, yourself—is always the greatest, most amazing thing since the invention of the iPhone. If you don't believe that, nobody else will.

But I was super happy to buy them because he was just so good: polite, super enthusiastic, and smart. He reminded me of, well, me!

I gave him the money and he left, and about twenty minutes later he came back. I answered the door and he said, "Mr. Sullivan, I'm very sorry. I overcharged you." He counted out the money and gave me back about $40, which I couldn't believe. This kid was amazing. His name is John Dominici, and he and I became friends. He's got to be eighteen or nineteen by now, and whatever he does with his life I'll bet he's a success at it. Hands down, he was one of the best pitch people I ever dealt with. I couldn't say no to him.

I knew that John had targeted me that day I was out running and said he was sorry about Billy to tug at my heart a little. But I didn't feel manipulated. I *respected* it. He had loaded the dice. He knew that if I liked him a little, I would let him in the door and he would be more likely to sell me. He was right. Try it.

WITH GREAT POWER COMES GREAT RESPONSIBILITY

But no matter how much you try to load the dice, a real pitching superhero goes into any pitch with at least some basic tools designed to help push back. Here are some of the most effective ones, many of which I've used myself.

- **Know your audience's expectations.** Before I sat down with Liz Smith, I knew she had a reputation for being tough. I also knew that if she criticized my business she would probably expect me to fold like a lawn chair. That insight let me decide how to flip the script on her by *refusing* to back down. That intrigued her and gave me an opening. Understand who you're dealing with and have a plausible idea of what they expect in a pitching situation. Do they expect humility? Brashness? An elaborate demo? A short speech? Formal dress? Shorts and flip-flops? The more you know about the other guy's expectations, the better you can surprise him or her by going against those expectations if you get pushback.
- **Do your research.** Flipping the script in the face of an objection or refusal might start with "I think you're wrong about this," but it can't *stop* there. Your comeback must have two other components: a realistic reason *why* they're wrong and a solution that proves your point. You'll only find your reason and solution if you know your audience extremely well. Do your research into the person or company. What mistakes have they made in the past and why? How can you solve a problem for them? Be specific. Because while "I think you're wrong about this" won't convince anybody, "I think you're wrong about this, because the media market is 400 percent bigger than the last time

your company was in direct response back in 2013" is pretty impressive.

- **Read the room.** Not everybody will push back as a test. Some people are just contrary. Somebody might be having a shitty day or be confused about what you're offering. Learn which by reading the room when you walk in. Is the person offering objections as a way for you to show what you know? Are you being tested? Or are you dealing with somebody who's at the end of her rope and just wants to go home?
- **Generate fierce agreement.** If you do a great job of suggesting an alternative or arguing your case, you might create *fierce agreement* (which I talked about a few chapters back). Fierce agreement means the other person becomes your collaborator and is totally in—physically, emotionally, mentally, spiritually and intellectually. Sometimes you get there by disagreeing with the other person. I will tell someone I think we need to reexamine the issue and have an open conversation about what's at stake.

This is something I learned from the street markets. You can tell when someone's 100 percent in because you've got them nodding, their money on the table. You could say, "We're going to sail across the Atlantic solo in a boat" and they would pump their fist and say, "When do we leave!" I cultivate that energy at my company. When we take a project on, I want people invested in it and emotionally excited about it, so it actually makes them feel good to think about it. That emotional engagement is everything. When you fall in love with someone, you're in fierce agreement, right? All the stars line up. You're completely together in what you're doing.

- **Know when to stop.** If you push back and offer a terrific collaborative approach and still get the stink-eye from the other party, it might be time to cut your losses and step back. There are times when you can push back and make a convincing case but be in a situation where the other person isn't in a position to agree to anything. In that case, offer up your reason and solution and then make a confident exit. The chips will fall where they may. Or if one person has already made their mind up and is starting to tune you out, you could do what I've done: stop my pitch, turn around, drink coffee, and talk to one of their co-workers.

Other occasions when this Pitch Power might save your butt include:

- **Getting an offer on anything.** Unless you have no choice, never accept the first offer for anything. Demand better terms for a loan. If someone makes an offer on your home, push back with a counteroffer. If you get a job offer, push back and ask for something more, even if it's an extra week of vacation. Even if the other party refuses, you'll gain respect.
- **Landing an interview.** Whether you're writing a blog, producing newspaper articles, or laboring over a school paper, odds are you'll want to interview someone influential or important. Trouble is, those people won't always cooperate. If someone refuses an interview, offer to go to their home, email them questions, or suggest that you'll just have to interview their archrival instead. Or simply call every day until they say yes just to get rid of you.

- **Getting a poor grade.** If you're in school, your work is your pitch. If it comes back with a grade that's not as good as you hoped, push back. Demand to know why you were given the grade and ask if there is anything you can do to bring your grade up. If your instructor likes you, there may be ways to turn a C into a B+.

Plot Twist!

There's a basic truth about getting what you want: no matter how super your Pitch Powers are, no matter how hard you work, reaching your goal is always, always going to be harder than you think it will be when you start out. That's true of anything in life, I think. Whether you're trying to get a ripped body, make your business profitable, or get a book published, you're always swimming against the current. It's never easy.

So with that in mind, my plot twist for this section is all about Anthony Sullivan's "Pushback Multiplier Rule." What on earth is that? It's my basic rule for calculating how much pushback you're likely to get from any pitching situation. That's good info to have, because it prepares you for how hard you're going to have to work to get the deal, the big tip, or the upgrade. In my experience, it's much better to approach a pitch overprepared because you assumed you'd be in for a fight than it is to be underprepared because you fooled yourself into believing it would be a cakewalk.

The Pushback Multiplier Rule is pretty simple and works like this: for each obstacle between you and what you want, plan on pushing back 100 percent harder, longer, or more persuasively to reach your goal. These are the kinds of obstacles I mean:

- There are more experienced/qualified people after the same thing as you.
- You've never done what you're pitching to do.
- You have multiple layers of bureaucracy to fight through.
- Your audience is recovering from a reversal or a betrayal.
- You're asking your audience to do something they've never done before.
- You're asking for an outsized wad of money.
- You're a completely unknown quantity.

Let's do the math. Say you want to bring your Pitch Powers to bear in getting a business loan so you can start the surf clothing company you've been dreaming about since college. You figure if you meet with multiple banks to find the right fit, bringing all your superpowers to the table, the process should take about two months. But that's probably not right because you haven't taken the Pushback Multiplier Rule into consideration.

First, you've never gotten a business loan before, so you have no business credit history. Second, you've never run a business before. Third, you're asking for $1 million, a lot more than apparel companies in your area get as start-up capital. That's three obstacles, which means that getting your loan is going to be about 300 percent harder than you thought. You should plan on 300 percent more pushback, 300 percent more hard questions, and 300 percent more hoops to jump through. But if you expect that, you can plan for it and not become discouraged when instead of two months, it takes six months for you to get to "yes."

Got it? Just know that it's never easy to get what you desire. You have to push back, be more creative, and work harder than you can imagine. Know that going in and you'll be fine.

WHAT WOULD BILLY DO?

Billy Mays here! I always loved it when someone I was pitching pushed back. It gave me info into what they were really looking for. That's how I want you to view pushback from your audiences—as opportunities. They don't want what you're offering? Great! What DO they want? What pain do they feel that you can fix? Remember, "no" is just "yes" misspelled!

Training Montage

I've already given you a lot of tips on how to get ready to push back, from doing a lot of advance research into their problems to knowing an organization's culture and what they might expect from you. But there's no easy, risk-free way to develop the confidence you'll need to use this Pitch Power. You just have to do it.

Get out there and pitch. Ask your boss for a meeting to discuss a possible promotion. Call your credit card company to argue for a better interest rate. Shop for a car and get ready to haggle like you've never haggled before. Even shopping a flea market gives you a good chance to push back when a vendor quotes you a price on something. Whatever it is, offer a lower price. What's the worst that could happen?

Understand that for most people, pushing back and flipping the script is not natural behavior. Haggling over price is normal and expected at street markets in the Middle East; it's part of the culture. But in the United States, we're taught to be well-behaved little consumers. It can be really tough to speak up and say, "No, I think I'd like to pay 20 percent less for this," and then stick to your guns in the face of all the objections. So test your wings. Try it. Haggle, dicker, negotiate. Ask for more. Don't accept no for an answer. The more you do it, the more comfortable you'll become.

But what will really get you excited is when you see how your skill and enthusiasm rubs off on someone else. I've seen people light up when someone pushes back creatively against their objections. You see it on *Shark Tank*: the sharks all sitting there with their arms folded, skeptical. They don't really want to hear the pitch. But when someone comes in with the right level of enthusiasm and a rehearsed pitch with humor in it, the right amount of value, and strong confidence that they are *the answer,* even these cynical people get excited.

Try it. You'll be amazed.

SCENARIOS FOR USING THE "PUSH BACK" PITCH POWER

Q: *You come into a pitch and the person is sitting across from you stone-faced, arms folded, looking like he or she is going to push a button and dump you into a pit of alligators if you make one wrong move. Treat it as a bluff or as the person's real mood?*

A: You have to treat it as a bluff, because if you assume that the person you're pitching to is a rage monster on a hair-trigger, you're going to pitch scared, and that never works. Assume this is passive aggression and remember, not everybody is demonstrative. Someone can love your humor and only crack a small smile. Do your thing and don't worry about it.

Q: *Someone you're pitching takes flipping the script off the table before you even begin, by saying, "You should know that any offer we make is final." If they make an offer, should you respect it or push back anyway?*

A: No offer is final. I don't care what anyone says. Most of the time, that's just a negotiating ploy. Make your pitch and see what their offer is. If you really want to push hard, before you're done, give them a number and say, "That's my floor, so if your final offer is going to be below that, let me know so we don't waste anyone's time." But when in doubt, always pitch from a place of strength.

Q: *You're planning to pitch a potential new client when you hear through the grapevine that they reject every idea presented to them as a matter of course. Cancel and save the man-hours or treat this as a chance to work on your own pushback skills?*

A: Always make the pitch. Everybody needs the practice time, and you never know. Maybe the story that they reject every idea is a red herring to weed out the weaklings.

POWER NUMBER NINE

NEVER BE CLOSING

Good for saving the day in landing cynical new customers, selling hostile prospects, getting compliance from rebellious offspring, and adapting to changing audiences.

WHEN WE LAST LEFT OUR HERO . . .

You were figuring out ways to screw your courage to the sticking place so you can push back hard and flip the script on someone who resists your powers. Most of the time it's great to refuse to take no for an answer, but there comes a time in every superhero's life when you have to stop fighting. This is it.

ORIGIN STORY

If there was ever a time that I learned to trust the power of the pitch, it was my first time ever using it, and I did so because I had no choice. There haven't been many times when I've had such overwhelming fear that I thought it was going to cripple me, but this was one. It was 1991, I was in Bideford, England, and I was taking care of my buddy Phil Clamp's T-shirt stand.

This gentleman pulled up opposite me and he was selling something called the Amazing Washmatik, a car washer with a bucket, a hose, and a scrubber. I started watching him do his patter over and over again. He would repeat his patter and then he would sell. Then he would wait for the crowd to clear and he would repeat the patter and he would sell. He made it look really easy. He made it look fun.

I got tired of hearing the same jokes over and over again, but then I started to count how many £10 car washes he was selling compared to what I was selling. I would sell one T-shirt an hour. He would sell twenty-five Washmatiks an hour. It didn't take algebra to know he was doing pretty well, and he was using techniques I had never even seen before. He was having fun, telling jokes—he was pitching.

I plucked up my courage, went over to him between tips, and said, "Hey, my name is Sully and I want you to teach me how to do what you are doing." Immediately, he said no. He flicked me off like a mosquito. I went back to the T-shirt stand with my sad face and told Phil what had happened. When I got to the market the next day, Phil told me he'd asked the guy, Mark Bingham, and Mark had offered to teach me—or try to teach me—how to pitch like he did and sell the Washmatik.

Mark gave me an old-school tape recorder and told me to record his pitch. So I did. Then he told me to write it down and learn it word for word. He was adamant about it. *Word for fucking word.* "Don't change a thing. Don't make it your own. I will only let you do this if you do exactly as I say."

That's pretty powerful, so I did. I learned it like a script, like learning Shakespeare. It was about two pages of copy and I had it on the visor in my car. Every time I stopped at a red light I would pull it down, read it, and put it back up again. I would drive, learn the lines, and repeat them over and over.

You're a pitching superhero by now, so can you see where I messed up here? Of course, it was completely unknown territory, but still . . . you're right. I didn't rehearse with the product, because I didn't know I should. You need to put yourself in the arena—wearing the sword, holding the shield, and fighting to the death. I didn't. I practiced the words while brushing my teeth. I washed my car with the thing, but I never parked the car in front of a big window and pretended I was trying to sell it to anyone. So when I showed up at the market, I was confident and blissfully unprepared. I watched Mark pitch the Washmatik like a master, and then at noon he threw it at me and said, "You're up. I'll be back in an hour. I'm going to get lunch. See what you can do." Then he disappeared. That was good in a way because he wouldn't be watching me, but now I was terrified.

Magic

I didn't know how to bally a tip or stop anybody who walked by. I knew the pitch but I didn't know how to get anyone's attention. Standing there like an idiot, I thought, *I can't do this.* I forgot everything. Everyone seemed to be staring at me; I had complete, paranoid stage fright. Then I thought, *Fuck it, I've got nothing to lose. Just do it.* At that moment, a gentleman came over and said, "What does this do?" Thank God. The perfect question. I was off.

I was terrible. I didn't know how to match the words and the actions the way I had seen Mark do it. Nothing was working the way it was supposed to because I just didn't know the dance: the words and movements and engagement, the mechanics of the thing. Somehow—I don't know if the guy felt sorry for me or what—I managed to go through the whole pitch. By the time I finished, I had a crowd of eight or ten people watching me. And then I realized something huge: they didn't know this was my first go. They had no idea. When I "went to the turn" (pitchman-speak for asking for the money), I sold one. It was a magical moment. *Oh my God, I sold one!*

Just like that, all my fear went away. It had worked. It was like an incantation. I had said these words—I'd ham-fisted them and said them all wrong, but I'd said them—and someone handed me a £10 note. That's when my whole career started. The fear was gone because I had done it. I had broken the ice and someone had said yes. I'd trusted the pitch and it had worked. *Welcome to the world, lad.*

I ballyed another tip and now I was getting more confident. By the time my hour was up, I'd sold seven Washmatiks. When Mark came back, he said, "How many did you sell?" and I'm certain he thought the answer would be zero. When I handed him the £70, he just stared at it like I'd handed him a pineapple or a baseball. Then he said, "Seven?"

"Yeah, is that good?" I said. "Did I let you down?"

He just looked at me for a second and then said, "Be here tomorrow at 8:00 a.m." That was the beginning.

THE REVEAL

I couldn't have made the people at that market buy from me. I wasn't experienced. I barely knew what I was saying or doing. I was almost having an out-of-body experience. That's the point. I didn't try to sell them, coerce them, or manipulate them. I didn't "close" them or "ask for the sale," like they tell you to do in every book and seminar on selling. I did my pitch and let it do its thing, and I stepped back and let the results happen. At some point, that's all you can do.

Remember Blake, the Alec Baldwin character from the movie *Glengarry Glen Ross*? In his "go to hell" suit and his $10,000

Rolex, rapid-firing obscenities at poor Jack Lemmon and Alan Arkin? This is what pitching looks when that guy describes it:

> A-B-C. A-always, B-be, C-closing. Always be closing! Always be closing!! A-I-D-A. Attention, interest, decision, action. Attention—do I have your attention? Interest—are you interested? I know you are because it's fuck or walk. You close or you hit the bricks! Decision—have you made your decision for Christ?!! And action. A-I-D-A; get out there!! You got the prospects comin' in; you think they came in to get out of the rain? Guy doesn't walk on the lot unless he wants to buy. Sitting out there waiting to give you their money! Are you gonna take it? Are you man enough to take it?

I love it, but I hate it. I love the performance, but I hate the impression of pitching that it makes: high pressure, manipulative, not giving a shit about anything but getting what you want. In a movie that might work, but not in real life. Sometimes, you make your best pitch but the other person doesn't like it. Worse, he or she feels manipulated despite your best efforts. That's when you've got to be totally aware of the vibe and tempo in the room and know when to stop pitching.

Blake says, "Always be closing." *Wrong*. This Pitch Power is about doing the opposite.

NEVER BE CLOSING

Don't push. Don't say, "What's it going to take to sell you this car?" There is a moment to stop pitching, shut up, and let the chips fall where they may. Your goal is to get what you want, but that's not going to happen 100 percent of the time, or even 50 percent of the time. But you know what can happen most of the time? The person you pitch can walk away feeling good about spending time with you. Most of the time, that means you stop trying to control things and give control back to the listener. You listen and learn and don't try to control the outcome. No one wants to feel worked or overpowered, and having the grace and sense to see that is a point in your favor.

In my world, the most important transaction I can be involved in is forming a good relationship with you. If I'm pitching you, I'm not interested in making a one-time sale. I don't want you to walk away feeling dirty and believing you've been ripped off. I want you to leave happy, content, and satisfied, even if you don't hire me or date me. I want you to leave with a story of someone who came to see you, made you laugh, and had some guts. I want you to remember me as a good guy who was trying to help, because while we don't wind up working together today, maybe a year from now you remember that I

THE PERSUADER!

Never be closing? But what about asking for the sale, getting the outcome you want? Remember . . . persuasion. If you do the pitch right, you won't need to ask for the result you want, mate.

The Persuader explains: "A great pitch makes the other party *want* to do business with you, buy from you, go out with you, or give you the deal or the job because you've made them feel good about being around you. That's why this is so powerful when it's done well. When you entertain, share, project confidence, and positive energy and solve the other guy's problem, you make him do what you want while thinking it's his idea. That's mind control without the creepiness."

was the one who didn't push too hard and you call me when another opportunity opens up.

Plus, at some point, continuing to press just damages you. You become the guy who won't quit hitting on the cute girl even though she's obviously not interested. You want to lean in and whisper, "Mate, you're just embarrassing yourself." Sometimes, the desk clerk isn't going to give you a discount on the room. The loan officer is not going to negotiate with you. Let it go. The idea is to win more times than you lose but not think you can win every time. A percentage of pitches are going to fail. I know, because they fail for me, too. Let them. How you handle the failure—the poise and confidence with which you process the fact that you *can't* control this encounter—will say as much about you as anything else you do.

Anatomy of a Superpower

What makes this Pitch Power unique is that it's less about what you do than about what you don't do. Don't press. Don't force the issue. Don't say something transparently salesish. The goal is to make the person conducting a job interview feel stupid if they don't hire you. What a powerful thing. Instead of you walking in and feeling like you're Oliver Twist asking Fagin, "Please, sir, can I have some more?" you can turn the tables. You make the person know he has to hire you right then and there, because if he doesn't, you're going to go and work for his competition.

Or maybe the girl is going to sit on her barstool and think, *I need to go out with this guy right now because he just blew my mind.* Or you'll be the teacher whose kids can't wait to go to her class because she's engaged them and has them loving the material and getting great grades. Or you'll become the car salesman who, instead of watching two-thirds of prospects walk away after a test drive and a pushy sales pitch, has the customers who not only buy cars but enjoy the experience and even refer their friends.

The key to this Pitch Power is a truth that seems so bloody simple but is so easy to miss if you let yourself get caught up in worrying about outcomes and commissions and all that other bollocks: *your audience isn't going to decide based on anything you say or do, but on how you make them feel.* Maya Angelou said, "I've learned that people will forget what you said, people will forget what you did, but people will never forget how you made them feel." That's 100 percent right.

Successful pitching isn't about facts and figures. It's about making your audience feel comfortable—getting them to know that they can trust you with their time, money, safety, reputation, whatever you're asking for. When you pitch a literary agent on representing your novel, you're trying to convince her that she can *trust* you to deliver a terrific book, be a professional, and not waste her time. When you persuade a bank loan officer to give you a great rate on a mortgage, you're really persuading him that you're a good person who can be *trusted* to pay back the money and not get him fired. When you close a sale, the customer *trusts* that the product will be as good as advertised and deliver the value you promised.

Where does that trust come from? Hell, this is all so simple when you strip away the salesy bullshit! Trust comes when your words, actions, and the whole person who shows up says this in big, bold letters:

I care about you and your well-being as much as or more than I care about my own.

The funny thing is, you can't say that or you'll sound completely full of shit. If you make a ham-handed grab for the sale like a dog lunging at a piece of meat, you're letting the person across the desk know that it really is all about the sale and you couldn't care less about them. That's why the pitch at this level is like jujitsu: you don't attack the goal directly, but indirectly. You say it with your sincerity, knowledge, attention to value and detail, confidence, humor, good ideas, and preparation. When the audience feels comfortable, when they like you, when they trust you—that's when you win.

How Not to Do It

Want to see examples of what not to do? Go to any clothing store, for starters. Department store salespeople are the worst. Everything looks good on you because they just want the commission. But ask them about Prada versus Versace and they look at you like you just asked them to explain relativity.

Car salesmen have a terrible rep and mostly deserve it. Pressuring you into buying by taking your trade-in car for hours and not giving it back isn't pitching. A great pitch doesn't make you hate the pitchman. Want a fun activity when you're feeling cheeky and want to screw with someone? Walk onto a car lot and after the jackals descend, pick out the guy who seems like the biggest jerk. Walk up to a Ford Focus and hear him insist, "You're a Focus person." Then change your mind and walk over to an F-150 and he'll go, "Oh, you're a truck person." Then try it with a Mustang. You can do this all day!

You also see it in waitstaff. I can't stand the ones who I know, no matter what I ask about on the menu, will say, "Oh, it's really good." Look, sunshine, not everything on the menu can be really good. I need you to help me out here, not kiss the chef's ass. Outcomes, outcomes, outcomes. When all you care about is the outcome, you lose.

So, what can you do to create trust and comfort while not closing?

Listen

Too many inexperienced pitchmen talk and talk until the audience is bored silly, and they don't even realize they're missing out on the best source of information about their audience: their audience itself. Often, verbal diarrhea is caused by nerves. A little bit of nervous energy is fine and normal, but nerves that make you blather on while the listener becomes glassy-eyed will cost you. That's why you practice your pitch.

Say your piece and then shut it. Let the listener settle in and absorb what you've said. Most important, listen to what he or she has to say in response. You can learn a great deal about what your audience needs, fears, or isn't getting from people. I've learned more about potential clients from listening to one of their people bitch about their other production companies than I ever have from formal research.

Listening comes with a companion skill: asking great questions. Don't just talk about yourself and what you have to offer. Learn about your audience and prepare two or three brilliant questions. Then when the time is right, ask them, maintain strong eye contact, and wait for the answers. Remember, people want to tell their story. If you let them, they will usually share even more than they intended.

Choose Silence

Are you one of those people who fears silence and tries to fill it with talk? Start doing what you must to become comfortable with silence, because it's one of a pitchman's most powerful tools. Many times I've sat across a desk from someone and finished my pitch and just let the silence settle in. They didn't talk. I didn't talk. But silence doesn't mean nothing is happening.

In silence, the other party can be absorbing what you've just told them. Their defenses can be dropping when they realize that you're letting some air back into the exchange. You can be thinking about what you're going to say or ask next. Also, when you get comfortable with silence, you give the other guy a chance to fill it, and what he or she says might be to your advantage.

But what I find most useful about silence is that it reboots the exchange. Everybody can breathe, step back, shake themselves, and then dive back into the conversation refreshed and ready. Finally, contrast is pleasing to the senses, and choosing silence after several minutes of passionate declaiming puts you in control of the pace and tempo of the conversation.

Offer Value, No Strings Attached

The best service providers I know—consultants, writers, lawyers—are more than happy to share what they know on the phone or in person with no obligation. That's smart. Obviously, they're not giving away the store or spending eight hours consulting with someone for free, but they provide tremendous value in letting a prospect pick their brain for a pleasant forty-five-minute Skype session. That makes a fantastic impression on anyone you're pitching, because you're essentially saying, "I'm giving you all this wonderful information without asking you to commit, and I'm confident enough that I believe you'll come back as a paying client when the call is over."

You know what? They're usually right. Giving someone value with no strings is an incredibly potent pitching technique. Let's say you're sitting across the desk from a recruiter for a highly regarded tech company. You've studied the company exhaustively and you have some terrific ideas for solving some of their IT security problems—and you share those ideas in your interview. You don't say, "I'll share my ideas if you hire me"; you share them to show the recruiter just what he could be missing if he doesn't hire you. Then you smile, say thank you, and walk out. If your ideas are strong, eight times out of ten you're going to get called back.

Before your next pitching opportunity, think about how you could create value for the other party. It won't work with every audience; you can't really create value for a credit card company or airline. But when you're pitching for a job, a client, or to get a reporter to write about your company, that extra value can be the difference between yes and no.

Collaborate

My favorite restaurant experiences are the ones where I walk in and ask, "What's good?" and the waitress says something like "These are my favorites, but just because I like them doesn't mean you will. Let's talk about what you like." I love that you're willing to be candid about your restaurant, because now we're co-conspirators in trying to find me a good meal. The server has shown me she cares and is honest—oh, and by the way, she's now completely in control of what I eat.

If you can find a way to turn the people you're pitching into collaborators with you, you're golden. Now you're working together against forces of evil. It takes things to a different, more intimate level and gives you opportunities to steer the encounter toward your goals. For the waitress, her goal is a big tip. To get that, she needs me to buy a $100 bottle of wine, because she doesn't share tips on wine with the kitchen. But

INCOMPETENT SIDEKICK: EGOMANIAC

Oy, the Egomaniac. He loves the sound of his own voice so much that he won't shut up long enough to let the listener get a word in edgewise. While that might be okay if you're delivering a TED talk and you're supposed to be talking for thirty minutes, most of the time this sidekick is the kiss of death. He'll bore the pants off your audience and make you look like a self-absorbed twit. Remember this rule: less is more. It's better to keep your pitch short and have your listener ask you for more info than talk and talk until she tunes you out. Kick Egomaniac to the curb and remember why you're pitching: to build trust. You do that by respecting the other person's time and intelligence, keeping it brief, and listening.

she doesn't sell me the wine; she sells me an experience that she curates and that we collaborate on. She knows if she can get me to order this dish, she can legitimately recommend that wine to go with it. She's not selling wine. She's selling trust: trust that the food she suggests will be great and that the wine will complement it perfectly. Maybe she even suggests that the people at a different table hated this wine, even though it's a ninety-six-pointer in Wine Spectator, but she thinks I'll appreciate it because, fuck them. She's gone from being a server to an advisor to an ally. She's made herself my personal food consigliere and I'm going to tip her magnificently.

The pitching superhero anchors the listener in the moment, not thinking about anything else. That doesn't happen when you're closing somebody.

WITH GREAT POWER COMES GREAT RESPONSIBILITY

At the beginning of my career, I was a twenty-two-year-old man holding a mop at a street market and telling you how I was going to make your life easier. It was a repetitious, not very glamorous job. People laughed at me and made fun of me. Hell, I would have made fun of me, too. But I was good at it, and it wasn't just about the pitch. If we're being honest, any idiot can memorize lines. I know because I did it. To really have success in connecting with people and building trust, you need to own what you're doing and love what you're doing.

I worked hard. I got ten times more rejections than sales. By the time I paid for my market space, petrol, and cheap food, I probably cleared £10. But I loved it, and it showed. I loved the products I was pitching, loved making people laugh, loved knowing that I was getting better and better as a pitchman. My goal was to infect people with my enthusiasm so when they saw me, it felt like the only reason I was there was to share my enthusiasm with them—*not* to sell them anything.

If you're going to really be a superhero at pitching, learn to love doing it. You have to love sharing what you know and sharing your story. You need to love your product, especially if the product is you. That way, you're not selling or closing. You're confident and excited and telling someone about something amazing in a non-Amway or "join my church" kind of way. Mark told me to memorize the words and actions and people would buy, but he missed something. I had to love what I was doing or it wouldn't have worked. The reason I sold seven car washers when he expected me to sell none was that, nervous as I was, I instantly loved it. The old saying "Do what you love and the money will follow" is true.

Pay attention to the flip side of this, too: don't ever pitch for an opportunity that you don't 100 percent want or pitch a product you don't believe in. If you do, you'll become nothing more than a closer and a salesperson. That's soul destroying.

Finally, as often as possible, go into every pitching situation with the mindset that you're there to serve. Again, that doesn't always apply, but more often than not it does. Let's say you're buying a car and hate car salesmen. But that pushy hack is trying to achieve a goal, which is to earn a commission fast without having a miserable time. He doesn't want to sweat you like an FBI interrogator to get you to buy a car; he might just not know another way. But suppose you go in with a service mentality and say, "This is what I want, this is what you want, so let's not play the usual games and you can walk away in an hour with a nice sale and everybody can be smiling, okay?" Now you're showing him another way!

A service mentality won't always land. Some people aren't interested in liking you or even listening. But this approach will show you who they are fast, so you can move on to a more receptive audience in pitch-perfect situations like:

- **Consulting.** Consultants frequently dig deep into the affairs of their clients, so trust is imperative. If you're a consultant and you want more clients, talk less and listen more. When you do speak, ask smart, concise questions and then while the prospect is answering, plan your follow-up questions. Be a fount of useful knowledge and resources so the prospect can't imagine living without you.
- **Financial planning.** The saying goes that a physician might know about a patient's habits and an attorney might know about a client's troubles, but a financial planner knows about *everything*. If that's your profession, your product really isn't picking stocks; it's trust. Listen, learn, and be the source of reliable information about all

things financial. Managing a person's entire financial life means being an ally, not just a service provider.

- **Reporting.** If you're a writer, journalist, or blogger, you're going to be faced with the task of getting people to talk to you who don't want to. Again, we're back to trust. If someone sensitive and guarded thinks you see them as the means to a story, they'll clam up. But everyone wants someone who will listen to them. Be a listener, not a note taker. That's what digital recorders are for.

Story-Furthering Interlude

Bishop Carlton Pearson knows a great deal about the power of service and commitment, particularly of listening. A renowned, controversial Pentecostal preacher and author of multiple books, his dramatic life story is the subject of a film that's in production as I write this: *Come Sunday*, starring Oscar nominee Chiwetel Ejiofor and Emmy winner Martin Sheen. As a charismatic performer and singer who speaks to huge audiences, Pearson believes that listening for and to the rhythm and vibrations of the audience and feeling how they change is the key to effective, meaningful communication.

"When I speak, I always stop and feel," he says. "Feeling is the emotional attachment and connection you have to the person or persons you're addressing, whether it's a crowd of five thousand or an individual. I'm always feeling out the room and connecting with the energy of the people listening to me. When I speak, I take the time to stay connected to the emotional temperature and I flow with that. Sometimes I'm the thermometer and other times I'm the thermostat, but I remain in control of the room as best I can.

"In any exchange, even when a single person is addressing a huge audience, there are always traffic signals," he continues.

"They are the emotions or commotions that flash just below the surface. When you're cruising along and talking without listening and without silences, you can miss them, just like you miss signs on the highway when you're going eighty miles an hour. But when you see everything as a conversation, there are a lot of intersections. Green is go: they love what I'm saying and want more. Yellow is slow down: something isn't working and I need to rethink or proceed with caution. Red is danger: it doesn't mean I should stop talking, but instead take a different approach, back up, put it in neutral, and watch what's happening . . . or needs to happen.

"The space between the words is the mystical part," Pearson concludes. "The best communication comes in the space between the words. You need to constantly be aware of the pulse of the conversation, whether it's long or short. Communication is as much about a feeling as it is about words and ideas. We spell words, but words also cast spells on us. A spellbinding speaker or communicator casts a spell or enchantment on the audience. Communication then becomes spirit to spirit.

Plot Twist!

For all that you might try to feel the room and listen, every now and again you will find yourself across the table from someone who insists on making your entire encounter transactional—what they have, what you want, period. When that happens, you probably don't want to be your noncloser self, because they're not interested. But that doesn't mean you can't pitch.

Suppose it's a job interview and the questions are the usual ones: Where did you go to school? What was your GPA? What do you think you can offer this company? What do you think your strong points are? What are you most proud of? But every single question is an opportunity to pivot to something else, to take control more directly.

I think every single question is a pivot point. When you get "What are you most proud of?" you pivot to "I'm most proud of the value I brought to my last employer and here's how I think I can do the same for you" or "I don't think what I'm most proud of is that important, but here's what I would like to do for you." When you get the classic clunker "What's your biggest weakness?" you pivot to "That's an interesting question, but I think my strengths are a lot more interesting."

If the other party isn't going to let you build trust and form an alliance, fine. But you can use Pitch Powers to steer even a transactional encounter back to how you can help, how you can create value, and how you're different.

There are even times when the best thing you can do is cut to the chase, be quick, and be ultra-transactional. For instance, when you're dealing with someone you know is extremely busy. They don't have time to chat with you for thirty minutes; you get three. Here's your shot, kid. Don't hit it into the rough.

I'm incredibly busy, so at Sullivan Productions I love when someone comes in, pitches me, and tells me in two minutes why I should hire them: "I work at Wells Fargo Bank and I'm bored. I want a friendly environment with more challenge, and I think television production is exciting. I see your company growing. I can do QuickBooks. I can do Excel. I can manage budgets. I can do quarterly reports. I'm on time. I'm quiet. I can take the trash out. I can communicate. I'm a great team member. I'm a self-starter. I show up on time, do my job, and don't gossip. I'm willing to learn. I'll work late, and I'll work weekends."

You're hired.

Know your audience and read the room.

WHAT WOULD BILLY DO?

Billy Mays here! I never needed to close because I painted pictures with power gestures, catchphrases, and lots of detail about my products. You can do the same thing, even if you're pitching a lender for a mortgage or a client for a new account. You're not just trying to sell a home, but a "classic Craftsman with leaded-glass windows and a Japanese garden." You're not just going to give the client wonderful service but "connect with them for weekly updates on our proprietary online workspace, where we can show you our latest drafts in real time." Wow them with details, then stop. Let everything sink in. And remember that some people, just to make it look you're NOT in control, will make you wait for their decision even though they're dying to say yes. Give them that. If you've nailed your pitch, they'll be back.

Training Montage

How? By practicing, as always. Most of us love to hear ourselves talk and tend to treat the time when we should be listening, really listening, as an interval when we're waiting to talk again. Plus, we speak too quickly and rarely pause. So . . . practice.

Go to social events and ask three questions of someone for every question you answer. Work on slowing down your speech until it sounds painfully, ridiculously slow to your ears. Trust me; it will sound quite normal to your listeners. Work on not jumping into the first break in someone else's speech to fill the pause with your own words; instead, let silence sit. If someone else fills it, fine. Pay extra attention to details like names, which many of us are terrible at remembering, and where people are from.

You can do all these things at parties, nightclubs, or professional networking events—consequence-free spots that are perfect for quelling any natural reflex you might have to make the conversation all about you. Most of all, learn to read the room. Does it feel boisterous and playful? Quiet and conservative? Profane and subversive? Tilt the tenor of what you say and when you say it to suit the room.

A great time to do this is when you're delivering a speech. Does your audience respond quickly to jokes? Do they nod in agreement? It's probably worth trying some audience participation. If they sit like stones, attempts to get them involved will probably fall flat. Public speaking is a fantastic training ground for pitching; if you haven't done it, try it. If you're terrified, as many people are, try getting involved in an organization like Toastmasters or learn from online lessons on free resources like Udemy and FutureLearn's Talk the Talk course.

Speaking is terrific because you're never closing. Your main goal is to convince, captivate, and inspire. That's superpowered pitching.

SCENARIOS FOR USING THE "NEVER BE CLOSING" PITCH POWER

Q: *You're at a sales meeting and the customer is clearly in sync with you, ready to buy. Do you go for the traditional "ask for the sale" move, or could you be sabotaging yourself?*

A: If you've built trust, then it's okay to ask for the sale. But do it in a way that's engaging: "Fran, this is the part in my pitch where I'm supposed to ask for the sale, but I can see that we're really having a good time and I don't want to screw it up by turning back into a salesperson. Do you think it's okay if I ask for the sale now?" Ninety percent of the time, you'll get a laugh, and the sale.

Q: *You've said your piece and so has your audience. Now there's silence . . . and more silence. Nobody is saying anything, and it's getting weird. Do you fill the silence or wait it out? How do you escape?*

A: Read the room, but I think it's stronger to wait it out. If the energy in the room is dying, you can perk it up by saying something completely out of left field, like "Y'know, I was giving away oranges to a bunch of triathletes one time . . ." Always fall back on making people laugh.

Q: *You're coaching a team (in sports or business; it doesn't matter), a leadership position where you're expected to be the main speaker. You want to open the floor to questions but don't want to turn things into a free-for-all. What do you do?*

A: Have everyone submit questions on cards ahead of time, like at a town hall meeting. Then answer the best ones.

POWER NUMBER TEN

FINISH WITH CONFIDENCE

Good for saving the day in sales, getting someone to call you, making an impression at a job interview, getting that raise or promotion, and making one hell of an exit.

WHEN WE LAST LEFT OUR HERO . . .

You were probably reeling from all the things I've told you, all the superpowers you secretly possess, and all the things you need to do to use them to get what you want in life. Not to mention that I just blew apart the whole "go for the close" ethos of traditional selling in about six thousand words. Mind blown? Well, hang in there because we're almost at the end. There's one more thing to share before you can go out and save the world.

ORIGIN STORY

In England, there was always respect for what we called the "barrow boys," the lads down at the street market who worked all day selling fruit and vegetables. We knew it was hard work. If you had the gift of the gab, if you had the balls to get up there and pitch, day after day, rain or shine, you were kind of revered in your community. These were the funny guys, the guys who made out at school. They were the Artful Dodgers of our world.

If you ever read or watched *Oliver Twist*, there was something about the Artful Dodger that everyone liked, even though you knew he was up to no good. He was cheerful, smart, had guts, and could charm a lady right out of her corset. You wanted him to succeed. What I liked about pitching was that it had this nostalgic, Britannic mystique about it. Nobody really knew what went on behind the curtains. It was a secret underworld.

But it was a hard life then, and it's still hard today. It's like being part of a band of gypsies: get up in the morning, drive to the location where you set up your stand, set up, go to work talking and persuading all day long. You're in a different town every day, like a traveling circus, but you work with the same people. There's a camaraderie around it. The pitchmen are one of the reasons why people go to the markets. You might go down to get your fruit and vegetables, but the reason you'd want to go is because of the hilarious, ballsy, "hang it all out there" guy selling slicers or potato peelers. Everybody loves a daredevil—if he survives.

When I realized I could do it, I loved being the center of that world. The success of the market hinged on the five or six pitchers out of a hundred vendors. The pitch joints were the ones that would draw the crowds, stop the crowds, and give people a reason to go to the market in the first place. Even if you ended up buying a car wash, a slicer, or whatever the hell some fast talker was selling, you didn't mind because the guy made you laugh. People got sucked in.

My dad was the worst. There was a guy selling these cheap vegetable slicers that didn't even work, but was great at pitching. I warned my dad, "Don't stand next to him." But he did. He said to me, "He's brilliant, this guy. He cuts the tomatoes, and he cuts the cucumbers, and he turns the potatoes into french fries in like two seconds." He bought one and we never used it. But that's the power of the pitch.

Why do people let themselves get sucked in? Fear of missing out, mostly. They also like having someone else in control, and like being mesmerized and dazzled. They like the sleight of hand. The great pitchmen have incredible hand motions because they've practiced for thousands of hours. Everything is designed to look effortless: pick up that potato while making constant eye contact, put it in the slicer (not even looking at the blade that will cut your fingers off if you don't pay attention), and out fall french fries by the bucketful. The great ones are able to deliver a perfect pitch blindfolded, freeing them to stare right into the other person's soul while they're pitching. It's theatrics, eye contact, hand movements, the voice, drama, and humor. It's all there. The best pitchmen have all of it.

The Blind Box

But the best of the best understand that in their hearts, people want to be tricked just a little, and they use that to make closing offers that are impossible to refuse. When I was working in Cardiff, Wales, I saw this guy (I don't remember his name) who had a thing called the Blind Box. He would pull up in a big eighteen-wheel truck, roll the side down, and it would be filled with whatever he was selling that day. If it was Christmastime, it was full of toys that he would auction. But what really blew my mind was the Blind Box.

He would pile up fifty boxes on the stage. You had no idea what was in them, and he would run his spiel: "It's a gift; it's not a cold cup of tea or a pork sandwich. It's not a villa in the south of France. What's in this box is a genuine gift. I can't tell you what's in the box, but here's the deal. If you buy this box, you cannot open this box here today. You have to wait until you get it home. If you do open the box and you look inside it and you're delighted with what you see, and the person next to you asks what's in the box, tell them to mind their own bloody business and buy their own box."

It was one of the most amazing things I've ever seen: the *irresistible offer* but with nothing behind it but air and intrigue. This guy would sell these boxes for a pound each, fifty of them, right there and then. Nobody had any idea what was in them, but they would happily part with their money because he had made a promise. You didn't even care what was in the box because you wanted to be part of the select few who got one. You got ripped off for a pound, but he made fifty quid. I always found it absolutely stunning that fifty people would go for it. I used to sit there in amazement and watch this guy sell fifty boxes. It was a big dog and pony show.

When he got to fifty, he would tell people to hold their boxes up, but not to open them, and people would do it. I never found out what was in the Blind Box. To this day, I still have no idea. In part, it's the mystery that's fun: the ability of the pitching superhero to bend people to his will—not only effortlessly, but to make them smile while doing it!

THE REVEAL

The Blind Box is all about the ability to finish strong, often with an offer that the other person can't refuse. If you don't have an offer, then it's about closing your pitch by making an impression that makes the other person remember you when he or she forgets everybody else. The Blind Box did both. Punters bought the box because of the allure of the unknown, the offer they couldn't resist. And some of them were so enamored of the mystery that they took it home and years later have *still never opened it*. I'm serious. That pitchman with his big rig and boxes is *still* mesmerizing those people years later.

When I talk about closing strong, I'm not talking closing like you close a sale. But I am talking about wrapping up your pitch in a way that compels the other person to act, even if they don't act until a week after you walk out that door. I'm talking about making an impression, or as we call this final Pitch Power . . .

Finish with Confidence

In psychology, there's a concept called the *peak-end rule*. It says that we judge an experience largely on two factors: how we feel at its most intense point (the peak) and how we feel at its conclusion. I can't speak for other parts of life or business, but in pitching, the peak-end rule is 100 percent right. You want to be at your best at the most intense part of the negotiation, meeting, or date, and at the end when you say farewell and exit stage left. Those are the parts of your pitch that will do the heavy lifting in persuading people to give you what you want.

Finishing with confidence isn't about asking for the sale, either. It's about ending with a flourish, something that makes the other person want to know more. It's Sully's version of the "when to leave the party" rule: better to leave a party too soon and have people saying, "I wish she was still here" than too late, so they're muttering, "She's so boring, I wish she would go home."

For our final lesson in Pitch Powers, I'm going to tell you how to make the kind of exit that sells, compels, and rings the right bells.

THE PERSUADER!

Flash is cash! Packaging matters, because after you walk out of the office, conference room, theater, or bar, the only thing your audience will have is the impression you made. Which is why the Persuader always dresses the part. That seems so basic, but not everyone does it. Everyone should.

The Persuader says: "When people don't know you, they'll treat you in accordance with how you package yourself, and your attire and grooming are the most visible parts of that packaging. Look the bloody part. Either have a standard uniform that you always wear in persuasion situations—like Billy Mays's blue shirt and khakis—or dress for the occasion. If it's a job interview, wear a suit. If it's a chat at a sports bar, dress down. But always be neat, groomed, sharp, and pay attention to the details of your appearance, from the length of your hair to the dirt under your nails. Fair or not, people will judge your capacity to manage big responsibilities based on your ability to take care of those small details."

ANATOMY OF A SUPERPOWER

Finishing strong doesn't just mean you end your presentation or speech with something memorable. Often, it means that by making a can't-miss offer or claim, you can end the pitch then and there—force the other party to decide, then and there. That's power.

When I first came to America in 1992, I was already a seasoned pitchman in London. But I came into contact with Jon Nokes, an expat who had moved to California, who saw something in me. I really wanted to pitch in America, so I said, "I'll come over. I'll pay my way. You do not have to pay me. I'll show up in LA with a smile on my face." He hired me to pitch at the Los Angeles County Fair, and I flew to California.

By offering to work for free and pay my way, I made it impossible for him to say no. I was going to be there. I wanted to work for him. He didn't have to pay me a salary because I was on commission only. He literally had nothing to lose. Already, he was impressed that I was twenty-two years old, and prepared to drop everything in England and travel across an ocean to a place where I didn't know a soul and sell mops with no guarantees. I made myself indispensable and attractive because I knew I could do it.

I'll spare you the details of setting up shop at the Antelope Valley Fair in the city of Lancaster, about an hour north of LA, where it was 115 degrees in the shade, with smog and desert wind that wouldn't quit. I'd never been so hot in my life. It was a miserable, back-breaking experience. Jon was testing me to see if I had the stamina to play in the big leagues, and I did. I actually made the *Los Angeles Times* after someone came out and interviewed me.

That story highlights one of the most potent parts of this Pitch Power: the "wow" offer. Offering to work for free, giving someone something special, or providing something that will solve a problem on the spot is an incredible way to build your credibility and set yourself apart from everyone else. Another variation of the "I'll work for free" gambit is something freelancers use: the free preview. If you want to land a desirable new writing, design, or consulting client, you say, "Tell you what, I believe so strongly in what I can do for you that I'll do a small initial project for nothing—no fee, no commitment. You don't love it, you keep it and you don't owe me a dime."

Who could turn that down? Of course, you have to attach conditions to that kind of thing or you'll end up bankrupting yourself with free work. But I've used that trick to entice new clients like HSN to my commercial production shop, and it works. By offering something free, you remove the risk. You also project massive confidence. Why would you risk hours and hours of unpaid work if you weren't sure you could deliver quality?

In a sales situation, the "wow" offer can also be a free giveaway item, anything from a sleeve of golf balls to a product sample. If you're a teacher trying to win over a classroom, you can give the students a free period to read or relax. If you're trying to convince someone to have dinner with you, one gambit might be saying, "I'll be having dinner at the Café Orléans next Friday at nine. If you show up and join me, I'll buy you a marvelous dinner. If you show up and don't wish to join me, I'll still buy your dinner. And if you don't join me because you show up with a date, I'll buy your dinner and his." Talk about confidence and élan!

Another time I used the "wow" offer to my advantage led to my big break as a producer and director. It was 1998, and I had been on-air talent for a long time, but I wanted to be a producer because I knew it would be more lucrative and open doors to more products. The problem was, it was pre-Internet and I had little to nothing to show for my new production company—no tools, no clips, no contacts, no reel. I took a page out of Robert Rodriguez's book, *Rebel without a Crew*, and made up business cards that read ANTHONY SULLIVAN with the word PRODUCER printed under my name. I was a self-proclaimed producer . . . who had never produced anything! I still had no equipment or experience and hadn't made any commercials.

Everyone I pitched on my "production company" pretty much laughed at me.

Then I talked to AJ Khubani, the founder of Telebrands (the "As Seen on TV" company) and the godfather of the infomercial. AJ intimidated a lot of people, but I figured if anyone would give me a break, it would be him. At the time, AJ had a product called the Rotato, a rotating vegetable peeler, and he approached me about appearing in a commercial for it that was being produced by someone else. I had been selling the Rotato on HSN and had been successful as the live pitchman, but while I'd been in several commercials, I had never liked the writing because it just didn't sound like me. The writers that were hired to write the scripts just didn't get it. They had never actually sold anything.

I took a deep breath and told AJ, "Here's the deal. I'll be in the commercial, but I want to write it, produce it, direct it, edit it, and star in it. And I'll do it all for $50,000." He was so blown away by my enthusiasm that he wrote me a check on the spot! The first independent Sullivan Productions commercial was for the Rotato, and it was a hit. That was my big break. I went into Telebrands with guns blazing, refusing to take no for an answer. I had never directed, produced, or edited anything in my life and I punched way above my weight because I said, "I'm going to do this." That commercial is why I'm producing today. That pitch changed my life. I went from pitchman to producer in five minutes!

Twenty years later, I've produced hundreds of commercials for AJ and Telebrands and we have one of the greatest working relationships and friendships that one could wish for.

Apart from an offer they can't refuse, there are five additional elements to this Pitch Power:

1. Appear not to need what you're pitching for. This is a next-level skill, because you've got to project the sense that you're not desperate. If things don't go as you'd like them to, you'll move on to the next thing, no worries. At the same time, you can't appear indifferent to the situation. One really effective way to do this is to be extremely candid in what you say. Don't be rude or obnoxious, but do not pull punches. In talking to an attractive stranger, be honest. Directness and candor suggest confidence and that you're not too worried about the outcome.

I saw one pitchman do something like this. His name was Andy Gilbert, he sold watches, and his pitch was a bit of a con. He would get his joint set up in markets, and then go, "Ladies and gentlemen, I don't need your money!" It took balls. In the market world, that's blasphemy. Then he doubled down on it.

He'd say, "In fact, I'm going to give £10 to the first person who can raise their hand, on the count of three!" I was sitting there, watching, thinking, Where's he going with this? Then he'd pull a £10 note from a massive wad of money in his pocket and wave it in the air. "I'll give £10 to the first lady who can raise her hand on the count of three!" Now he had everyone's attention and had ballyed a huge tip. He'd count, "One! Two!" But he wouldn't do three. He'd mess with people:

"You were cheating."

"Stop picking your nose."

Meanwhile, everyone was laughing and more people were coming over seeing the hands in the air. Finally, he'd go, "One! Two! Three!" and a hundred hands would shoot up. It was impossible to pick who was first. So he would pick one woman and say, "Lady, you're the winner. Come on over here." When she went over, he would ask, "Are you a good girl? Are you a good girl? Are you a good girl? Come here, are you a good girl?"

Over and over again. Meanwhile, she and everyone else would be laughing hysterically. He'd ask the crowd, "Ladies and gentlemen, is she a good girl?" Then he would ask her husband or boyfriend the same.

Finally, she'd reply, "Yeah. I'm a good girl." At that, he would tuck the £10 note back in his pocket, say, "Good girls don't take money from strange men," and carry on. Everyone laughed at the joke, and nobody ever got upset.

By telling them he didn't need their money and then even offering to give them money, he gained his audience's trust and entertained them to boot. Andy also sold a lot of watches.

2. Make yourself invaluable. Say you're interviewing for a job or meeting with a potential client. You research their company, find that they've been having trouble filling a key finance position, and before you leave the meeting, you hand the person in charge a list of three highly qualified candidates as a suggestion. You've shown initiative, the ability to find information, and the desire to be a resource. Drop the mic on your way out.

When you can show the person across from you that you can solve problems, get things done, or do what no one else can—during your pitch—you make yourself extremely attractive and hard to turn down. You can be a source of valuable information, a connection to important people, or someone who comes up with a solution to a tough problem on the spot. It's even better if you do it with aplomb, a sort of effortless "no big deal" attitude. That says, *You need me; I do this every day. I am an assassin.*

3. Make an exit. When you're done with your pitch, how you leave the stage is as important as how you entered. First, have a closing line that you rehearse, so you don't stammer or hesitate. If it includes a call to action ("I hope to hear from you next week"), so much the better. Map out your exit route with your eyes so that when you get up from your chair you can walk out in a single, fluid motion. If you haven't handed out a business card yet, flash one or more quickly and seamlessly from the pocket you planned to keep them in.

Shake hands with the most important person first, making eye contact with everyone. Succinctly tell whoever you've been speaking to how wonderful it was to meet them, and confidently stride out. Try walking out the door backwards; it lets you maintain eye contact and control of the situation. If someone opens the door for you, thank them. Even better, if someone moves to open the door for you, open it for them instead. Boss move.

Mustn't-do moves for an exit: apologizing for anything you said or did (it projects weakness), offering the person a gift (which can be seen as ass-kissing), and trying to deliver a witty closing line as you exit (those almost always land with a thud).

4. State why you want this. Too many people go into any kind of pitching or persuasion situation hopeful, but not confident. That's the wrong attitude. You need to be clear about why you want what you're after. That's not the same as being entitled to something; none of us is entitled to a damned thing. Be assertive, be calm, but be direct. Let's say you're pitching for a raise:

"Boss, I really feel that I deserve a raise. I am committed to the company. I really love working here. I want you to know that I am going to continue to grow the bottom line. I love being part of the team and I'm not asking for a lot. If you

INCOMPETENT SIDEKICK: SAD SACK

The opposite of confident, Sad Sack spends all his time apologizing and making excuses for . . . well, everything. If you let him, as soon as you walk in the room to make your pitch he'll apologize for everything from your clothes to your voice to being eighteen seconds late. At a moment when everything hinges on you being confident and in control, this wimpy sidekick will wreck your entrance and make a cool, memorable exit impossible. Leave him and his excuses in the lobby.

could increase my wages by 5 percent, I would be absolutely delighted. I'd also like to have my health insurance covered." Tell them what you want. Don't leave it open ended or be coy.

Also, make it all positive. You may intend to leave your job if you don't get your raise, but don't tell your boss that. No one responds to threats. Instead, make them realize that you are a valuable asset: "I'll take on new responsibilities. I am happy to work more hours." That won't guarantee a yes, but it makes it hard to say no.

5. Be patient. Despite all this, you won't always see the fruits of your confident close right away. In fact, most of the time you will need to wait—and expecting that can often work in your favor. If you state your case, make your offer, and effect a slick exit without expecting anything more, people can't help but be impressed. Give them time to absorb what you said and did, time to meet with others who make you look even better, and time to think. Make sure they know how to reach you, and bide your time. If you pitched well, results will come.

WITH GREAT POWER COMES GREAT RESPONSIBILITY

In pitching (and this is true of most ventures in life), confidence really is everything. If you're able to project that elusive sense that you are in every possible way *the shit*, and the other person is daft if they don't cast/date/buy from you, you become infinitely more persuasive. But it's one thing for me to tell you, "Hey, pal, be confident." It's another thing entirely for you to possess the kind of confidence I'm talking about. Sure, confidence on the joint or in any other persuasion situation comes through years of doing: making mistakes, trying stuff out, and sheer repetition. But you don't want to wait ten years to have superpowers; you'd like to be able to do something amazing *now*. Right?

Fair enough. When it comes to finishing with confidence, become a triathlete. That perplexed look that just crossed your face tells me I need to explain, so I will. As I write this, I'm trying to gain entry into the 2017 Ironman World Championships in Kailua-Kona, Hawaii. If you know anything about the triathlon, you know that's the holy land of the sport, where the Ironman was invented. For a long-distance triathlete, "going to Kona" is like making the pilgrimage to Mecca for a Muslim: something you plan for your whole life. But it's not easy to get into the race. There are only so many slots for amateur "age groupers" like me, and the main ways in are winning a certain qualifying race or a lottery system. Right now, I'm trying everything I can to get a slot, but here's the thing. I have to train for the race—140.6 miles of swimming, biking, and running—no matter what, so that if I get in, I'm ready.

That means I have to do the right things without worrying about results, day after day—and *that*, my friend, is the key to finishing the pitch with confidence. For me, training has to be about the training, about getting stronger and faster and fitter, because I have no idea if I'll get into Kona. The training becomes the reward, and if I keep that mindset and I do get in, I'll be ready to finish. If I don't . . . well, then I'm fit enough to do another Ironman distance race that will qualify me for Kona in 2018.

Adopt the same attitude in your efforts to persuade people to give you what you want and you'll be successful. Delivering a spectacular pitch should *become* the point, not the results. Do your preparation, control the situation, breach that force field with your humor, turn your mistakes into gold—and don't worry about what happens. The pitch itself, when you do it right, is pure joy. You become an actor at center stage when the lines flow through you, a singer when every note lands. It feels awesome, and when your only goal is to put forth a fine-tuned, funny, commanding pitch that feels good to you, you *will* finish confidently.

The pitch *makes* you confident, because you know you can do something most people can't. You can stand up in front of one person or ten or five hundred without fear, deliver strong words and gestures and ideas and offers *without fear*, and move them to take action. That's what presidents and great leaders do. When you know you can do it, and doing it is enough, that's . . . man, that's a superpower.

And sure, you want to get the job, get the sale, get the girl or guy. You might even need to in order to make a living and pay your rent. I understand. But train your mind not to think about the result, only the pitch. Make it honest and compelling and perfect. Care about nothing else, then walk away. Trust me, if you can do that, you'll leave people gasping in your wake, wondering, *Who in the hell was that?* Not all of them will buy or hire you, but none of them will remain unmoved. That kind of mic-dropping finale works really well in these specific situations:

- **Acting.** Whether you're auditioning or actually doing the part, thinking only about your performance and not worrying about the audience will make you better. When you're acting only for yourself, you'll make bolder choices without fearing what the people watching will think.
- **Speaking.** Deliver your speech for yourself, not your audience. You can't control how they will react, so don't try. If you speak honestly and in a way that reflects your passion and commitment, they'll feel it, and they'll respond in kind.
- **Dating.** You know all about the effects of desperation, right? It's a killer whether you're out for a quick hookup or a long-term relationship. No one's interested in somebody with that "D" scarlet letter on their forehead, but everybody's interested in the guy or gal who doesn't seem to need anyone, is totally self-possessed, and has it all going on. Confidence is everything in the dating scene.

Do what feels right and act like outcomes don't matter, and they won't. Not because they don't matter, but because more of them will go your way.

Plot Twist!

One of the most important parts of finishing with confidence is knowing when to shut up. You must develop a sense of when the pitch is over. Because when it's done, it's done, even if you're not done, and you have to calibrate your rhythms to say what you need to say before the other person shows signs of tuning out.

But there is a time to stop pitching, period. Billy Mays was a very different person when he wasn't pitching. When we were on a plane, for instance, you would never know he was there unless he wanted you to. We'd have a beer and a low-key chat and that was it. He was super quiet. When he decided to go for the jugular vein, everything changed; Billy would turn you upside down and shake the money out of you. But he knew when to shut it off.

Some people never develop that instinct, and not knowing when to finish can really undermine you. There's a woman at HSN who sells a fitness product, and she's really talented, but she can't turn it off. She's pitching 24/7. I've sat next to her on Southwest Airlines flights and she'll be pitching the people seated next to her. You see their faces; they're in hell. Of course she sells some, because people buy to shut her up.

Ending your pitch with confidence means you've left the other person wanting more. You will never do that if you insist on getting through every bit of what you have to say—or worse, waiting until they look at their watch. Develop your instinct for knowing when it's time to shut up, say, "I think it's time I shut up," and shut up. That's your mic drop. You're done. Fold your hands in your lap and wait. If they want you to say more, you'll know.

Training Montage

Pitching is basic. It's human communication with all the social media bullshit stripped away. It's not science. The bottom line is, if you're going to approach this with the kind of overpowering confidence that will get you across the finish line, you have

WHAT WOULD BILLY DO?

Billy Mays here! Confidence was never my problem, but I wasn't always that way. I don't think anybody comes out of the womb dripping with confidence. Confidence comes from three things in my experience: knowing you're supremely prepared, knowing you can handle whatever surprises the situation throws at you, and knowing that you look, sound, and smell your best. That's why I always wore my blue shirt and khaki pants—because I looked good in them and never had to worry about what to wear. But when you're confident, that's where the love comes. I smiled while I was pitching because even though it was hard work, I loved it. I loved it because I was good at it! Virtuous cycle, baby.

to love it. You have to really, really love talking to people, making them laugh, touching them, and solving their problems, even for a second. That means you have to get past your fear. I can teach a timid cash register person at Publix, who's so petrified that she can barely bag groceries and talk to a customer, how to pitch. Give me six weeks with that girl and I'll have her out on the front lines at a home show selling like a pro. Why? Because once she sees that she can do it, she'll fall in love with *being able* to do it—with the *power* of doing it.

Finishing with confidence so you don't need to close anyone means *becoming* someone else. Once you experience the buzz, you want more and you fall in love with it. You become someone more poised and more self-aware of how your body and voice and actions affect others. You get a sense of your own power to get what you want, and when you do that, you can't help but be confident and love pitching. We all have it. Harness it and use it.

Think about the last time you watched a great bartender at work. He's having a great time because he's killing it—and he's killing it because he's having a great time. The enjoyment has to come first. You need to enjoy what you're doing. If you're the bartender and you're back there thinking, *How do I get bigger tips?* you're going to come across as manipulative. If you're really enjoying what you're doing, the tips always follow.

At a real bar—not a sports bar or restaurant, but a pub—what's the bartender doing half the time? He's not making drinks. He's cracking jokes. Chatting people up. Asking questions. Giving the regulars shit. "Hey, Bill, how's it going? How's your wife and my kids?" That sort of thing. It makes you smile even to be on the edge of that, because it's authentic human connection. And yeah, the patrons buy drinks and tip the barman and all's well, but they don't do it because he's trying to get them to tip. He's pitching them, and they don't know it, and the bartender might not even know it. But he's connecting, making them laugh, breaching the force field of new patrons—doing the whole thing. And he loves it. So they love it.

Confidence begets love begets confidence, but it starts with getting out there, doing it, and realizing, *I can pitch people and not die. Awesome.*

It requires work. You have to hustle. You've got to be into it. You're not going to do anything if you're sitting on your ass. But it's worth the effort. You'll become a more confident person, earn more money, and have a better life. You'll be happier, not only because you're getting the results you want but because you went out and got them. Too many people wait for life to come to them; pitching is about going out and grabbing what you want.

Get out there. Give away orange slices, twirl a sign, hand out flyers, tend bar. Find some way to reach across the terrifying empty space between you and other people: tell a joke, make them smile, and connect.

Practice. Practice, practice, practice.

Know your acceptable outcomes, and if you don't hit any of them, come up with new ones. I didn't know what I was doing in the beginning, and neither will you.

Get online and watch legends like Ron Popeil and Billy Mays do their thing. If you're having trouble getting to sleep, watch yours truly sell steamers or mops or OxiClean. You'll be out in seconds.

Go to home shows and markets and butcher what you can.

Find mentors like great salespeople who'll share what they know.

Join Toastmasters and learn how to deliver a speech even though your knees are trembling, you're sweating buckets, and your heart feels like it's about to pound right through your chest.

You can do this. You can pitch.

Now, go do it.

SCENARIOS FOR USING THE "FINISH WITH CONFIDENCE" PITCH POWER

Q: *You're finished with your pitch and you're about to make the perfect exit when the party you're pitching stops you and wants to ask more questions. Make an excuse and end things or sit back down?*

A: Leave. A great exit means you stay in control. Tell them you have another appointment and politely make yourself scarce. Always leave them wanting more.

Q: *You start to see the signs that you're losing your audience—fidgeting, checking the watch—but you know you can wow them with the last part of your pitch. Keep going or hit eject?*

A: It doesn't matter how great your close is if the audience is looking longingly at the exits. Wrap it up, even acknowledge that they might be looking a little bored—remember, self-deprecation is a powerful tool—and let them know you're more interested in their welfare, not hearing yourself jabber.

Q: *You make a mistake in your exit—heading for the wrong door, dropping your business cards, that sort of thing. Do you own it and make fun of yourself or just get out of there as soon as you can?*

A: You should know this by now: own it and make fun of yourself. The more you can laugh at yourself, the more they'll laugh with you, like you, and want to give you a chance.

GO USE YOUR POWERS FOR GOOD!

Where I live, we have a terrific professional soccer team, the Tampa Bay Rowdies. Earlier this year their owner, Bill Edwards, a real estate developer and billionaire who's also a friend and neighbor, invited me to go to New York with him and former St. Petersburg mayor Rick Baker to pitch Major League Soccer (MLS) on letting the Rowdies join the league as its eleventh team. It's a good fit: the Tampa metro area is the country's eleventh-largest media market, we have great fans, a great stadium, and more. So in January, Bill, Rick, and a whole traveling circus headed for the Big Apple (I couldn't go) to pitch Mark Abbott, deputy commissioner of the MLS.

Later, Bill told me what he did and I was impressed. See, Bill's a pitchman who made his fortune pitching VA loans to veterans. He wasn't about to write a letter or do a PowerPoint. When Bill does things, he does them big. He showed up in a Gulfstream jet with twenty people, including Ralph's Mob, the Rowdies' support group; the team mascot, Pete the Pelican; some dancing girls, and a dozen community leaders. He even flew in with a crate of Florida oranges, and took out a billboard in Times Square—it was an overwhelming charm offensive.

At the time this book goes to press, I won't know if the Rowdies will be joining the MLS or not. But it won't be for lack of trying. Bill blew their minds, and that could be the difference. He told me later: "Sully, I pitched the hell out of 'em!"

That's the point. Even a billionaire who can afford a $150 million franchise fee needed to know how to pitch. He knew his audience, made an entrance, broke down that force field, and more. It excited me, because it's validation of everything I've said. It doesn't matter how much money you have. It doesn't matter how much power you have. At the end of the day, you have to know how to *persuade*. Everybody needs to know how to pitch.

The learning never stops, either. I hope you're motivated to keep working on your Pitch Powers even after you put down this book, and I hope you'll share your progress with me. Here's how we can keep in touch:

- **My website, www.anthonysullivan.com.** This is the first place to go. Here, you can subscribe to my email list and get all kinds of exclusive bonus learning materials that you won't find anywhere else. You can check out my "Pitch Powers" series of instructional videos and use those quick lessons to hone your own skills. You can find out where I'll be speaking or doing a book signing. You can even sign up to get alerts about special pitching competitions I'll be holding in the future.
- **Facebook.** My Facebook fan page is facebook.com/Anthony Sullivan. I invite you to like my page, but also to send me a video of you giving me your best pitch. I'm always looking

for great pitching stories, so pitch me! If I love your pitch, I'll share it with all my readers and fans.
- **Twitter.** Go to twitter.com/sullyontv and give me a follow.
- **YouTube.** Find me on YouTube and you'll find all of my pitching videos and a lot more fun, silly, and interesting stuff. When you're on TV as much as I am, strange things are bound to happen.

Reach out anytime. Tell me about new Pitch Powers that I missed. Tell me about pitching tricks you've discovered or amazing things that you did with your superpowers. Ask me questions and I'll try to answer them. But whatever you do, don't stop working on your pitch. You can have everything you want if you know how to persuade the world to give it to you.

ACKNOWLEDGMENTS

Billy Mays was the king. If Billy were still walking this earth, we would be happier and the world would be a better place. He would cut through the nightly television craziness like a sharp knife with a pitch, a product, an offer too good to refuse, his booming voice, black beard, and blue shirt catching you off guard as you consumed your television nightly news.

You miss him, don't you? I miss him.

I didn't like working with Billy Mays. I *loved* it. I was never happier than when I was tapping on a laptop, he would talk, and the words would spew onto the page! We couldn't have been more different, but as two pitch guys we had so much in common. We were fiercely competitive and dedicated to the art of the pitch and making the sale. We wanted to be loved by our customers for entertaining them, making them laugh, and making the sale.

We would work rain or shine, indoors or out, home show, boat show, county fair, state fair. We both came up the hard way, selling $20 at a time, only he was from Pittsburgh and I was from England. Between us we had *much more* than the proverbial ten thousand hours on the box. When the TV cameras finally pointed in our direction, it was no accident that we blew up on TV everywhere.

Prepared, poised, and ready to pitch, Billy had a flow, a cadence, a volume and style that were all his. No one could do it like Billy. As we collaborated over the years, culminating in our show on Discovery Channel, *Pitchmen*, my respect for him as an artist (because that's what he really was) grew exponentially. When I think of Billy, my mind wanders, and then I smile.

Each script started with the same phrase, the ubiquitous "Hi! Billy Mays here!" Whenever I typed it, I knew that if he was sitting next to me, we would create TV magic. He was loud, he was proud, he was a winner, and he was the people's pitchman. He was no one-hit wonder. Billy could make nothing into something and then something *big,* time after time, without skipping a beat. He was a father, my friend, and the greatest pitchman of them all. I miss you, Billy. I know you had a book in you and this book—my book—is dedicated to you and the book you never got to write. Long live your laundry!

Of course, I owe a lot to some other people, too:

- To my dad, for believing in me and pushing me to do and be more.
- To my mum, who has always been there for me. You have both given me roots to grow and wings to fly.
- To my little brother, Mikey.
- To my amazing daughter, Devon, and her mum.
- To my friends Stuart, Jeff, Skip, Hauser, and the boys from Cooper Construction for never letting me lose sight of who I am and where I come from.

In business there have been too many to thank, but I'll try:

- Mark Bingham, Jon Ash, and Andy Gilbert for teaching me how to pitch.
- Simon Selkin for giving me my first big break.
- Jon Nokes for inspiring me to come to America.
- AJ Khubani for rolling the dice on me.

- Gretchen for my green card.
- HSN for giving a snot-nosed English kid a break and for sticking with me over the years.
- The entire OxiClean team, especially Matt, Britta, Bruce, Dan, Katie, and Cindy, for everything.
- Jennifer and the Nutrisystem Team—let's keep rocking!
- Assemblyman Paul Moriarty for guidance through turbulent times.
- Thom Beers and Discovery Channel, you are a rock.
- Nancy Kuni, I'm glad you found me.
- Steve Jones, I love you.
- Juls, thank you.
- Kern, keep up the pressure.
- Some of the greatest women anyone could ever know: Joy, Mindy, Rhonda, and Eliana.
- Bill Edwards, you're a diamond!
- Mishele, Keith, David, Dave, Ethan, Judy, you know who you are.
- The staff at the Ashram. You've kept me sane!

To the trailblazers and old timers (some of whom aren't here):

- Al Spino, Ron Popiel, Joe LeBeau, Swedish Mike, Wendy Wow, Tommy Motosko, John Moltino, Tim Evans, Kevin Gilbert, Colleen, Kris Morris, Ruby, John Florell, Wally Nash, Samantha, Annie, Carmine.
- The late Earl Greenburg, Roger Pliakas.
- My inner circle: Arwen, my assistant Veronika, Carla, Pete, Sug, Bryant, Paula, Cynthia, Noelle, Craig, and Ashley, and the entire team, including the hundreds of

people at Sullivan Productions who make it happen every day.

Most of all I would like to thank the punters—the customers! The hundreds of thousands of people from all over the world that have ever felt compelled to buy from me. To anyone and everyone wherever who has ever bought anything from me, thanks for the hours of fun you gave me trying to convince you that "I've got what you need" or "You need what I've got"!

Special thanks—

- To Tim Vandehey, my co-author. I could not have done this without you.
- To AJ and Poonam Khubani for your friendship and mentorship and some great bike rides.
- US Masters Swimming
- St. Pete Masters Swimming

INDEX

ABOUT THE AUTHORS

ANTHONY SULLIVAN is an entrepreneur, producer and pitchman best known as the spokesman for OxiClean. Sullivan is a popular TV personality, regularly seen on HSN and various commercials. His production company, Sullivan Productions, Inc., produces TV commercials for consumer products. He lives in St. Petersburg, Florida.

Learn more at AnthonySullivan.com

TIM VANDEHEY is a bestselling ghostwriter and co-author. He lives in Kansas City, Missouri with his wife and daughters.